THE NATURAL
BABY FOOD
COOKBOOK

UPDATED AND FULLY REVISED

THE NATURAL BABY FOOD COOKBOOK

MARGARET ELIZABETH KENDA
AND
PHYLLIS S. WILLIAMS

AVON BOOKS ◆ NEW YORK

AVON BOOKS
A division of
The Hearst Corporation
1350 Avenue of the Americas
New York, New York 10019

First Avon Books Printing: April 1973
First Avon Books Trade Printing: September 1982 (revised edition)

Library of Congress Cataloging in Publication Data:

Kenda, Margaret.
  The natural baby food cookbook.

  Bibliography
  Includes index.
  1. Cookery (Baby foods)   2. Cookery (Natural foods)
1. Williams, Phyllis.   II. Title.
TX740.K46 1982   649'3   82-8843
                      AACR2

CONTENTS

PART I

PART II

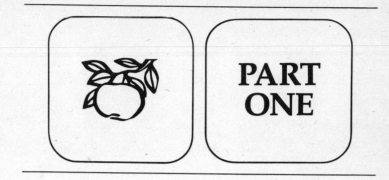

PART
ONE

NATURAL (AND UNNATURAL) FOOD FOR YOUR BABY

Your baby deserves natural eating.

A baby needs fresh wholesome foods even more than the rest of us do. Your own home cooking gives your child a fair first run at a healthy life.

Even though commercial baby foods are better than they were in the past, they remain overrefined, overprocessed, and overpriced. They are still a long way from being natural.

Like all convenience foods, commercial baby foods are expensive. You can use the best fresh ingredients for your homemade foods and still save perhaps seven times the cost of food from the factory.

Making baby food yourself takes only a little time, a small effort, and routine equipment.

You know what goes into your own foods. You have control. You don't depend on the uncertainties of the billion-dollar, profit-conscious baby food empires.

True, the baby food industry has been responding to pressure from its nutrition-minded customers. The changes have been slow, but with time they have come about.

A few years ago, we—like many other parents and professionals—were distressed by the ever-growing evidence that commercial baby food was just not good enough for babies.

A baby dining on commercial baby foods was deprived of the best available nutrition. Yet at the time, most babies were eating factory food from the time they were just a few weeks old.

3

Babies were getting far too much sugar, salt, starch, and other possibly harmful additives—and downright inferior foods.

Feeding your child the baby foods and junior foods you found on store shelves was, in effect, like giving the adults in your family a TV dinner every night.

How have things changed?

PROFITS IN BABY FOOD

The baby food industry continues to be a high-profit enterprise. It is the second most profitable food business.

Gerber Products, the H. J. Heinz Company, and the Beech-Nut Foods Corporation are selling baby foods to the tune of billions of dollars. Between 1978 and 1979, Gerber profits were up 20.6 percent, Heinz profits were up 14.4 percent.

Beech-Nut is reportedly doing just as well, but Beech-Nut does not disclose the figures. It is wholly owned by the Nestlé Corporation, based in Switzerland. Swiss corporations are a bit like Swiss bank accounts in their low profile.

Gerber holds the largest share of the U.S. market in baby foods, with sales at $334,987,000 for the fiscal year that ended March 31, 1980. You can find Gerber baby foods in 95 percent of the nation's major supermarkets.

So the baby food companies have been, to say the least, hanging on against their many attackers.

THE ATTACKS

The attacks became serious in the 1970s. The companies might have been able to brush off a few angry mothers, a few observant medical people and nutritionists, even a few natural foods writers like us. But the attack soon went beyond the opinions of ordinary people.

In 1970, *The Chemical Feast*, a Ralph Nader group book about the Food and Drug Administration, brought the first major complaint. The Nader study, coordinated by James S. Turner, explained that the inflation of food prices after World War II caused baby food companies to stretch their products with sugar, starch, and plain water.

Then probably in an effort to bring back some of the thinned-out taste, the companies added salt and monosodium glutamate (MSG). Like many another food processor, the baby food makers used preservatives and food colorings with abandon.

The first *Natural Baby Food Cookbook* came out in 1972. Thousands of mothers believed us and began making their own baby foods.

Next came the Consumers' Union information that supported our arguments against commercial baby foods. A number of other books were published, and the various publications appear to have stung the baby food companies into reaction.

At least, they were prepared to come to a verbal defense, even if they didn't want to change the ingredients of their baby food jars. The defense was based mainly on cleanliness. Commercial baby food, however inferior or full of additives, was at least sterile—that is, until you opened the jar.

Of course, home cooking also sterilizes food. A mother who prepares her own natural baby food starts out with it sterilized by the heat of cooking. She might let it spoil afterwards, or she might be careless enough to contaminate it. But then again she could open a jar and let that food spoil, too.

And, in fact, there is still some risk that dirt from the underside of the lid or from the outer jar might enter the baby food even as she opens the jar.

THE DEFENSES

The baby food company spokesmen found themselves in a sorry position. Against all reason, they had to defend excessive amounts of salt and sugar and preservatives as somehow desirable.

Robert A. Stewart of Gerber Products appeared on CBS television with Betty Furness several years ago, and was driven by these necessities to announce that "Sugar's an excellent food." He remarked, truthfully, that sodium (salt) occurs naturally in food and that "other factors" besides salt might cause hypertension in infants. But then, illogically, he used those remarks as a reason to claim that the high salt content of baby foods was "satisfactory."

And it's always possible, he said, that sugar doesn't absolutely always cause cavities in one's teeth. A scientist knows an exception or two to every rule, and any person of philosophical persuasion knows that nothing can be proved 100 percent true forever. So no doubt he was speaking as an objective scientist when he announced that sugar had "no clear tie-in with dental caries." He did not mention the other clear disadvantages of too much sugar in a baby's diet.

According to Dr. Stewart, all these taste-enhancers were, in any case, added to baby foods just to please mothers. As Dr. Stewart pointed out, there is "no reason why mothers shouldn't be pleased."

During most of the first year, in fact, babies simply cannot identify tastes that well. Babies can distinguish sweet tastes from sour, possibly even before they are born. But during most of their first year, they probably cannot tell any difference between salty and bland, and they have no way of knowing what food is spoiled, undercooked, or overseasoned.

It's up to the parents to distinguish good food from bad, unspoiled food from spoiled. Babies are likely to eat just about any food that doesn't strike them as sour—at least, at first.

In a television debate with one of us, a spokesman from the Heinz company showed that he was thinking of factory efficiency as well as the necessity to please mothers with the baby food products. He pointed out that sugar helps give baby foods the right texture for getting them into the jars smoothly.

Beech-Nut Corporation reacted to the persistent public relations problem even more bizarrely. In 1976, the company sent letters to more than 700,000 new mothers in an effort to scare them into using commercial baby foods.

In the letters, Beech-Nut claimed that home-cooked baby foods, such as spinach, carrots, and possibly beets, may (by a complicated process) cause a baby to turn blue and to stop breathing.

The danger, according to the Beech-Nut allegations, was that home-prepared vegetables may contain nitrates. Under certain conditions, nitrates can convert to nitrites. "Nitrites," the letters warned, "combine with red blood cell pigments in a manner which prevents these pigments from performing their job of transporting oxygen to the body. With too much methemoglobin, baby's skin turns blue and asphyxiation could result."

This rare condition is called methemoglobinemia. And though this condition has been seen, infants started on solids after five months of age do not develop it from vegetables.

The letters' scare tactics were based on no direct research. Beech-Nut admitted that the main source of information was a newspaper column by Jean Mayer, the country's best-known nutritionist. Dr. Mayer replied that his column was grossly misrepresented. His name was not cited in the letters. No other research was documented, either.

Although Beech-Nut did not say so in the letters, the only recent cases of methemoglobinemia had been in unusual circumstances—and all overseas.

A consumer-affairs agency in Syracuse, New York, demanded that Beech-Nut apologize to the new mothers for what the agency director, Roberta Wieloszynski, called "medical mumbo-jumbo." The American Academy of Pediatrics responded negatively, also, and the Consumers' Union had already come out in favor of the baby foods parents make themselves. So did the Center for Science in the Public Interest.

Beech-Nut claimed that the letters were simply a public service from a "responsible corporate citizen." The mailing, however, contained testimonials and coupons for Beech-Nut baby food products.

In the letters, Beech-Nut also claimed that parents who make baby foods at home risk bacterial contamination, food poisoning, and loss of nutrients through blending in too much air, pouring off water-soluble nutrients, freezing and thawing foods improperly, and using stale food. Beech-Nut failed to point out the easy solutions to all these problems—if they really are problems.

Later in this book, we outline the precautions that parents do need to take in making their own baby food. The precautions are not time-consuming or difficult, and they do keep parents from being exposed to unnecessary fears for their children's safety.

Eventually, Beech-Nut was forced to withdraw the letter and to issue apologies.

Clearly, some changes were in the air for the baby food industry. The attacks had reached the level of a corporate crisis.

The baby food companies continued to prosper, but they were well aware of their problems. They diversified. Today, a good proportion of the Gerber profits arise not so much from baby food sales as from other baby products: clothing, nursers, accessories, even vaporizers and humidifiers. Gerber began to take an interest in insurance and possibly future products for elderly people.

So, too, some increase in baby food sales came about automatically not because each mother was buying more but because there were more babies to buy for. The sons and daughters of the original postwar "baby boom" were giving birth to a second "baby boom."

Overall, the irate customers did seem to be having some effect on the industry's pocketbook. Public pressure was on for more nearly natural and safer baby foods, and, to some extent, the baby food companies had to act rather than just argue with their opponents.

THE IMPROVEMENTS

Monosodium glutamate (MSG) was the first questionable additive to be removed from commercial baby foods.

Under pressure from Senator McGovern's hearings in the Senate Select Committee on Nutrition and Human Needs, the manufacturers of MSG admitted that they had not conducted sufficient tests on the safety of their product as a flavor-enhancing food additive. Neither had the baby food companies.

By October 1969, the baby food companies voluntarily stopped putting MSG in their products. They argued that such tests as existed were "inconclusive," and in a standard industry reaction, they stated that their only reason for going along with the ban on MSG was a bow to public opinion.

Even so, we found MSG in some baby food jars for sale up through 1973. But the MSG is gone now.

And now, salt is out of most commercial baby foods. Most nutritionists frown upon giving a baby any naturally very salty fresh meat, much less deliberately adding table salt. Yet for years, baby meats contained perhaps as much as five times the salt that fresh meat contains.

Commercially strained vegetables had been known to contain as much as 60 times the salt of fresh vegetables.

Sugar is out of many commercial baby foods. The dessert products are still sweetened, as well as a few others. But previously, almost every baby food was sugared, and sometimes heavily sugared. Even the naturally very sweet apple and pineapple juices were often processed with extra sugar. Those "empty" calories, of course, were taking the place of superior foods.

Sugar itself is harmful. There is nothing good you can say about sugar, unless you consider pure non-nutritious calories a benefit.

Because a baby's taste is just developing, we ought to be helping

8

him to develop an appreciation for natural, fresh tartness in food rather than for constant oversweetness.

The baby food companies have helped by eliminating sugar in almost all their foods. (It is probably not entirely unfair to note that the sugar went out about the same time that sugar prices inflated so rapidly that sugar no longer qualified as an inexpensive filler.)

Many of the artificial flavors, food colorings, and harmful preservatives are out.

A few varieties of commerical baby food are also without the modified starch. Starch is not especially nutritious, certainly not as a substitute for meats, vegetables, and fruits.

The Consumers' Union study said that manufacturers begin with tapioca or cornstarch and then modify it in order to speed up the processing. The manufacturers denied the motive. But modified starch does keep factory food from separating. You don't find a watery layer on top of the food, and you don't have to stir it.

For a long time, the companies also modified the starch in baby foods so that a baby's saliva would not digest it. Otherwise, the small amount of saliva left in half-eaten baby food would continue to "digest" the rest of the food in the jar so that it would quickly appear to be spoiled. The mother would throw it out and presumably might not be in a frame of mind to buy any more.

Now if the baby's saliva cannot digest the modified starch, it may happen that the rest of the baby's digestive system can't either. Dr. Thomas A. Anderson resigned his post as chief of the Heinz Nutritional Research Laboratory because the company would not act on his recommendation to remove the modified starches from baby food.

It is always wise to check the ingredients before you purchase any commercial food, especially on "combination" dinners. But most of the modified starches have been removed by this date.

In short, we have reached an era when the baby food makers are anxious to appear concerned with nutrition.

Heinz sends out brochures with details about nutrition. As part of its public relations program, Beech-Nut is instituting an advisory panel on nutrition. Yogurt now holds a certain cachet as a natural food, so Heinz introduced seven kinds of fruit yogurt.

All the companies now indicate a clear month and year deadline for using the contents of each jar. The undersides of the jars are

FDA-approved nontoxic, unchippable plastic coatings. The lids are made so that you can tell at a glance if the sterile seal has been broken.

The companies now make a point of listing the varieties of baby food that contain no sugar, no salt, or no preservatives.

Over the years, the baby food manufacturers have been slow to respond to the demand for better nutrition and better safety. They have showed themselves in a somewhat absurd light in their initial reactions to the demands.

But now we give them their due. They have improved the product greatly.

They also have their other points. They continue to offer an astonishing variety of foods. The variety is one way they make their profit, and much of their research is directed at new varieties. Gerber Products sells 150 choices in baby food, with 11 types of juice alone. Heinz comes in with 108 types of food.

If you like variety, you've got it. (Of course, many of these contain ingredients which are not particularly good for babies— chocolate and cinnamon, for example.)

When you are traveling with a baby, the commercial foods may be safer than homemade. They may be desirable in places where the food or the water supplies are uncertain.

Some elderly people buy them as convenient soft foods.

So do we hereby take back our enthusiasm for natural, home-made baby foods?

No!

THE CONTINUING
ADVANTAGES OF MAKING
YOUR OWN BABY FOOD

Factory-packed foods are just not as beneficial for your baby as the good, clean, nutritious foods you can make yourself.

And, certainly, the factory foods are not economical.

Often the home preparation of baby food takes no more time than it would have taken you to pick the jar off the shelf and pay for it in the first place, and the expense of the home food is often close to minimal.

How long does it take to mash up an inch of banana? Yet at this writing, the cost of a jar of strained bananas is the same as more than 1 pound of fresh bananas.

If you make your baby's food, you will be using up the leftovers immediately and profitably. That spoonful of peas, the last carrot stick, the extra pork chop will make up into a surprising amount of puréed baby food. Instead of good bits of food going into the garbage or, worse yet, into stale and unappetizing leftover dinners, you will find they will do for an instant and complete meal or two for the youngest member of the family.

You cut down waste.

You save money.

You don't pay half again as much for softened foods (like applesauce, for instance) in jars especially marketed for babies as you would for nearly identical foods in jars sold for adults.

If you make your own food, you pay virtually nothing for the main additive of much infant cuisine. This main additive won't do any nutritional harm, either. It's water. Water is the major ingredient in about 40 percent of the many varieties of commercial baby foods. Liquid would be a major ingredient in your own softened baby food, too. But at least you won't be paying a meat-and-vegetable price for plain water.

Commercial baby foods are even more liable than other canned foods to one kind of vitamin destruction. Most are offered for sale in clear glass jars in well-lighted supermarkets. The light shining through the glass destroys vitamins B_2 and B_6. Even stove-top cooking in clear glassware results in some loss of these vitamins, because of light damage.

The shelf life of commercial baby foods is somewhat shorter than it used to be, since many of the preservatives are out.

But there is time for damage.

The handling of a crop from the time it is harvested until you get it to your table affects the nutrient value. The longer the food is stored, generally, the more food value will be lost.

How does it strike you that your baby may consume meat many times older than he is, or vegetables that ripened in some unknown season past, or fruits whose time in the jar runs into years?

If you begin with fresh foods, you can at least avoid some of the more than 3,000 artificial additives that have entered processed foods. Any food you buy is subject to some kinds of damage. But you have more chance of getting the best food values when you

11

buy the freshest and least processed you can find. You don't have to doctor up homemade food so that it can be sold and shipped and shelved for prolonged periods of time.

We ought to be suspicious of food that does not spoil, the bread that does not get stale or moldy. If it is not good enough for the normal deterioration processes to take place, as brought about by living plant and animal organisms, it is hardly good enough for your baby or you.

Some of the baby food industry practices are standard in food-processing industries, but they are not appetizing, and their effects on nutrient values are simply not known. Fruits and vegetables, for instance, are peeled with lye. Lye peeling cuts labor, but how does it change the ultimate food product?

In almost every instance, you can substitute superior ingredients and superior preparation.

You can eliminate sugar and much of the starch. You can avoid extra salt. You can use whole-grain flours and fresh produce. You can replace the inferior foods that are for filling rather than for growing.

Food is the most important pleasure in a baby's life. It means rocking and cuddling. It is physical ease from the cramping and grinding of an immature digestive system.

Of course, the baby loves milk. Of course, the baby eagerly eats bland and milky, smooth-textured baby food. It tastes more or less like what the baby is used to.

That may be all right during infancy. But suddenly you may find the baby is two years old and feeling all the contrariness of two-year-old people, and you can't get away from the bland baby foods. The baby is growing up, but still wants nothing at all but the long-familiar milk and the purées of the baby food jars. The growing child has not learned how to chew. The taste of ordinary table foods seems exotic. Variety, tastes, textures in food appear distressing rather than pleasurable.

As children with this attitude get bigger, they are liable to like only foods that are bad, bad, bad for them. They will want only the bland flavors that speak of overrefining, oversweetening, and overprocessing, that don't speak of good nutrition.

They may even start getting fat on a diet of cereal, cookies, bread, and sweets, with only an occasional hamburger thrown in.

It's a common problem in America. The baby is naturally curious about food. Food is a chance to explore, a bit of an adventure. But a toddler can forget the adventure for the tasteless purées, sweetness, and starch of the commercial jars.

This is one of the best reasons for doing your own cooking for your baby from the beginning.

Your own food tastes better. It teaches better. It has bright natural colors and real tastes. Your own chicken-and-carrots dinner is guaranteed not to taste the same or look or feel or chew the same as the fish-and-peas dinner of the previous night or the beef-and-squash meal for tomorrow.

As the months go by and the teeth come in, you can make the baby's food ever chewier and lumpier and more varied. You don't want your baby to sit passively and eat one insipid mixture after another. The textures and smells and colors of your homemade food will have your baby at the top of the class in dexterity, in feeling independent, in being accomplished and happy with the world.

Besides, you won't be tempted to overstuff the baby to finish off a set number of ounces in a jar. It won't be 4½ ounces of baby food or 6¾ ounces of junior food later.

If you make your baby's own food, too, you can build around the adult menus your family likes best. Your child will quickly be eating adult foods at the table with no series of jumps in weaning from "strained" to "junior" to "toddler" and then to table foods. The baby will grow to eat the same variety of foods as the rest of the family. You won't be caught in the position of having a child who has developed a taste for jarred turkey, while the older members of the family reserve turkey for Thanksgiving only.

If caring for your baby makes you try such nutritious foods as liver and spinach on the adults more often, that is all for the best, too. You may find your own nutrition improving as you try out for yourself what's good for your baby. In your concern for a balanced diet for your baby, you will undoubtedly be caring more for a balanced diet for yourself.

Perhaps good infant nutrition is not, on some levels, a matter of life and death. But good nutrition makes a real difference in trouble spots. Good nutrition can be crucial for a baby who is sick or weak. And it can make the difference between routine borderline health in a baby and the real vigor and strength that we would all like to see in our children.

CHAPTER TWO

MOTHER'S MILK AND MILK FORMULA

It's not nice to fool Mother Nature.

Formula companies, after all these years of trying, have been unable to fool her. Human milk is still better for a baby than any other formulation people have been able to come up with. It's common sense to nurse a newborn baby the way Mother Nature intended.

If you need more than common sense to tell you so, you could look at more than fifty scientific studies. The American Academy of Pediatrics looked at the studies and has begun a campaign to promote mother's milk as the ideal for human infants. Both boys and girls, the Academy says, ought to be learning about breast-feeding in school. Government programs ought to be making it easier. Doctors, nurses, dieticians, and hospitals ought to be using their immense powers to promote it.

Employers, the Academy says, should be allowing longer maternity leaves, and they should set up at-work child-care centers so that mothers can take a nursing break along with their coffee break.

COMPARISON OF HUMAN AND COW'S MILK

Essentially, most of the ordinary formula substitutes for human milk are based on cow's milk. We call them by the word *formula* because they've been modified in a laboratory, but they are still mostly derived from that base of cow's milk for calves, not humans.

Why isn't unmodified cow's milk good for a human baby?

Right after birth, a calf can stagger to its feet and find its milk. In a few months, it has all the education it needs to be bovine or bullish, as the case may be. So if you compare human milk to cow's milk, you find that cow's milk contains more than three times the protein of human milk. Big Mama Cow is giving her baby protein enough so that in two years, the calf will be all grown up.

Human milk, in contrast, contains nearly twice the carbohydrates of cow's milk. The baby does not need to be running around the meadows in two weeks. Instead, the human baby needs to complete a complicated nervous system and, with luck, a powerful brain. The carbohydrate and fat content of human milk allow that sort of slow, complex growth.

Human milk and cow's milk have about the same fat content, 3.5 to 3.8 percent, but the fat in human milk is more digestible for human babies, and contains just the right balance of fatty acids for completing the central nervous system.

Obviously, human beings are tough animals. They've taken over the world. And one physical reason is that their digestive systems can tolerate abuse. Even the immature digestive system of an infant can usually put up with cow's milk.

But an infant digestive system must work hard to cope with the excessive protein of cow's milk. The excessive protein puts stress on the baby's kidneys. The curd form is larger and harder in cow's milk and less digestible for babies. And cow's milk protein can sometimes cause slight bleeding in the intestines and lead to a form of anemia.

In the best of the commercial formulae, cow's milk is modified to resemble human milk as nearly as possible. The American Academy of Pediatrics recommends formula for babies who are not breastfed. For most babies, formula is safer than is plain cow's milk. The protein in formula is changed so that it will form a softer curd in baby's stomach and will digest more easily. Carbohydrates are increased in proportions similar to those in mother's milk, and the formula is fortified with vitamins and minerals, usually including iron. Vegetable oils are added to formula to repeat the most essential fatty acids.

Plain cow's milk contains about four times the salt of human milk, so formula manufacturers must reduce the salt as well.

Still, the amino acid "building blocks" of the protein are a different type. (The amino acid in cow's milk is mostly casein; in human milk, it is mostly lactalbumin.)

And still, cow's milk or cow's milk formula forms an odorous stool. To be blunt, breastfed babies smell better than bottle-fed babies. Breastfed babies hardly smell any worse than a little cheesy.

It is not that the scientists have failed to create satisfactory substitutes for human milk. They have identified most of the components of human milk, and they do a good job of modifying cow's milk insofar as it can be modified. But they can't create human milk out of cow's milk any more than they could make a living tree out of scrap lumber.

ADVANTAGES OF BREASTFEEDING

Laboratory formula is consistent and uniform in its ingredients. That's only right for a commercial product. Mother's milk, on the other hand, changes as the baby changes. One way of looking at it is that breastfeeding is a continuation of pregnancy. A mother's body provides for the varying needs of the fetus as it develops, and lactation varies for the same purpose.

It's a different milk for a baby who is one hour old than for a child who is one year old, old enough to eat other foods and to lose some of the early dependence on mother's milk.

Science has to have its limits when it comes to duplicating all that. We can't grow a baby in a decanter, and we can't formulate perfect human milk.

New milk for a newborn baby is called colostrum. For most animals, colostrum is a life-or-death matter. A dairy farmer would give up on a calf that received no colostrum from its mother within twenty-four hours after birth. Human beings can survive without colostrum, but it has immense benefits.

Colostrum helps to clean out the digestive system in the first days after birth. It provides extra immunities for the newborn baby.

After the first few days, the colostrum slowly departs and gradually gives way to the mother's milk that is meant to nourish the baby through the next months of growth.

Both colostrum and the regular human milk contain antibodies that protect infants from intestinal disease and diarrhea at a time when they are most vulnerable. The breastfed baby runs less risk of diaper rash because the stool is acidic, and the acid discourages the growth of bacteria that cause diaper rashes. Cow's milk produces a neutral to alkaline stool in which these bacteria multiply.

During the nursing period, breastfed babies have fewer illnesses than do bottle-fed babies. They tend to suffer fewer staph infections. They are less liable to catch the common influenza, ear infections, and respiratory infections that their older siblings may bring home from school. If they do come down with one of these illnesses, it may be less severe than it might have been.

Statistically, bottle-fed babies suffer eczema seven times as often as breastfed babies. Those who are not inoculated run more danger of contracting such serious illnesses as polio, encephalitis, mumps, or meningitis. The Sudden Infant Death Syndrome (often called crib death) strikes bottle-fed babies more often than it strikes breastfed babies, although no study has established any provable connection.

An important benefit of mother's milk is the lower incidence of allergies. Babies are almost never allergic to human milk, but they frequently develop allergies to cow's milk.

The list of potential benefits goes on and on.

Breastfed babies tend to be normal weight—or if they do get fat, they usually recover normal weight without difficulty by the time they are toddlers.

One reason that bottle-fed babies can get fat is that they may continue to suck on the bottle after they are no longer hungry. The breastfed baby may nurse just "for fun," too, but in the course of a nursing, as the first rush of milk subsides, the baby takes in fewer and fewer added calories. At that point, the nursing is more for pacifying and for satisfying the sucking instinct than for gratifying hunger.

Dental studies show that babies fed at the breast develop fewer problems with their teeth than do bottle-fed babies. Breastfeeding is work for the baby, and the natural sucking develops the baby's mouth, jaw, and gums in the right way. In the future, you may save thousands of dollars on dental work and orthodontia.

Breastfeeding may save you hundreds of dollars because you won't have to buy formula, bottles, bottle liners, and sterilizing equipment.

Some authorities have even advanced the theory that breastfed babies have less difficulty in learning to read when they reach school age. The reasoning is that the nursing mother switches the baby from one breast to another, instead of holding a bottle at the most convenient side. This constant changing from side to side may lead to better eye coordination and better visual learning.

Occasionally, nutrition experts report finding traces of environmental chemicals that have entered human milk. These may be the all-pervasive pesticides like DDT, or chemicals that have entered the food and water supply from illegal dumping of industrial waste, chemicals like polychlorinated biphenyls (PCBs) and polybrominated biphenyls (PBBs).

But the benefits of human milk still far outweigh the unknown, theoretical risk presented by the pollutants, which may or may not enter the milk of any individual woman.

So far, no baby is known to have been hurt by contaminants taken in from breastfeeding alone.

Remember, too, that most milk formula must be diluted, and thus, with formula, you depend on the local water supply even more directly than you do when you breastfeed. With formula, you also run some risk of bacterial contamination, or the water might contain nitrates or a high amount of sodium or some other potential problem that cannot affect mother's milk.

Of course, you never have to worry about sterilizing your own milk.

Several years ago, one of us was busy fussing over the breastfeeding of the firstborn son, and a neighbor was extending her sympathy. She thought nursing mothers were nothing less than heroic. "It must be," she said, "so painful to sterilize the milk!"

Fortunately, a nursing mother does not need to boil bottles, much less anything more sensitive.

And there are other benefits for the mother. You may remember the old jokes about how mother's milk doesn't take up room in the refrigerator, and it's easy to take on a picnic, and it's never too hot or too cold.

There are, of course, many emotional benefits for the nursing mother. The hormone responsible for releasing milk is prolactin. Besides helping to create milk, prolactin also brings about maternal feelings. It makes a mother feel close to her baby.

It is interesting to note that some scientists have considered the farfetched possibility of injecting prolactin into attacking armies (presuming that they'd stand still for it). The idea is that they'd learn to love us instead of bombing us.

The hormone works on roosters anyway, if not on Vikings. If prolactin can make roosters brood over chicks, it can certainly help an exhausted mother to tolerate—and love—a crying baby in the middle of the night, when she needs all the emotional help she can get.

In the first hours, days, and weeks after the birth of a baby, breastfeeding helps the mother get back into shape. The system seems miraculous at the time. Each time the baby suckles, oxytocin is released into the mother's bloodstream. Oxytocin causes the uterus to contract rhythmically. The contractions close off the open vessels left by the expulsion of the placenta. And they force out the last remnants of the endometrium, the soft lining that nested the fetus in the mother's uterus. As she nurses, the mother can feel her abdomen pulling back into some semblance of flatness.

Now one of the most delightful benefits of breastfeeding is that it helps the mother lose the extra weight she may have gained during pregnancy.

In fact, nature intends some of the normal weight that a mother ought to gain during pregnancy as a reserve against the demands of breastfeeding. She can lose the weight as she nurses, even without dieting.

Look at it this way: A nursing mother is likely to be providing her baby with more than 20 ounces of milk a day. An average ounce of human milk contains about 20 calories. So the day's milk comes to 400 to 600 calories in all. Essentially, these calories come from the mother. She needs 400 to 600 calories a day just for the milk. In addition, the body functions to produce the milk, and that internal activity burns up more calories, about 400 more a day.

So the mother needs an extra 800 to 1,000 calories a day just for nursing.

Most likely, she will rapidly go back to what she weighed before pregnancy. And if she wants to lose more weight, this is a good time for her to do so without a restrictive diet. She is working hard at nursing, taking care of the baby, and doing the other jobs that make up her life. She doesn't need to starve to get her waistline back. She can lose weight and eat normally at the same time.

By "normally," we do not mean that a nursing mother can afford to go on banana-cream pie binges. For her own sake, and for the baby's welfare, a nursing mother needs extra protein, calcium, vitamins, and minerals. She needs a good, natural, balanced diet.

She does not dare to get used to eating for two. As time goes on and the baby grows, she will be eating for one again—and, if she continues to feel entitled to the nursing mother's ample diet, she could be one fat person.

CONTROVERSIAL ISSUES

We fully recognize that breastfeeding, for all its benefits, is sometimes not easy in the modern world.

Over the years, the media have certainly become explicit about other intimate sexual matters. The double-entendre has become the open dirty joke. Advertising can get crude. Even prime-time television takes a frank attitude toward sex—a bit giggly, but candid.

Nursing is another matter. Once in a while, one sees a nursing mother sitting miserably in a smelly public rest room so that she won't offend anyone with the sight of her baby nursing. A woman who wears a bikini in full sight of everyone on the beach will sit under three blankets with her baby.

Times are changing, and the modesty issue is not so much of a problem as it once was. A mother can learn to nurse unobtrusively.

But a few women still feel embarrassed about nursing. Some husbands are even more embarrassed by the idea. And the general public still gets surprisingly nasty about the very idea of a nursing toddler.

Breastfeeding may be overly controversial for a sensitive new mother. For every woman who announces in near fury that she wouldn't be caught dead breastfeeding (an unlikely possibility), there seems to be another woman aggressively nursing a four-year-old as if she were saving the world.

Sometimes everyone seems to be pressuring the new mother. Infant backpacks sport buttons that assert "I'm a breastfed baby." Some mothers, who feed their babies with cow's milk, whisper that their breastfeeding colleagues are nothing but cows.

On some levels of society, bottle-feeding is prized because it demonstrates that the parents are wealthy enough to afford formula, and it seems to show that the parents are scientific and precise. On other levels of society, it is avant-garde to nurse, a sort of clever counter-cultural move.

Even the professionals get in on the controversy. One doctor believes that breastfeeding spoils babies and makes them disobedient and "un-American." Another crusader says formula feeding is "criminal."

This unkind controversy is not limited to our own society. It is said that in parts of Africa where the medical missionaries take in orphaned babies, the townspeople sneer at the orphans for having no human soul because they had no mother's milk.

HUMAN MILK AS A
NATURAL RESOURCE

In the Third World, breastfeeding is an important natural resource. Of course, the American mother who bottle-feeds is wasting resources. She is spending extra money, using up extra milk and extra hot water, and she is consuming extra implements. She is throwing away her own good milk. But presumably the waste is not a matter of life and death.

In the Third World, however, the mother who lets her milk dry up is courting starvation for her infant. The mother who uses an uncertain substitute brings closer the disease and filth that destroy so many children.

Mother's milk has actually been counted as a form of national wealth in some countries. Where food is scarce, the human mother is an important source of nourishment.

Yet the controversy of bottle-feeding boils over there, too. Companies like the Swiss-based Nestlé come in with modern advertising and modern temptations. Then they promote formula in the Third World by giving away free samples. Saleswomen dressed in white (who may or may not be nurses) arrive at maternity hospitals to sell formula. If the mother becomes dependent on using the free samples from another, more glamorous world, she runs the risk of losing her own milk supply. And buying formula represents one more impossible demand on her limited supply of money. Formula, in fact, is much more expensive in the Third World than it is in the countries of origin.

The older children are hungry, too, and they may steal the baby's formula. Or the mother may have to stretch out her supply by diluting it excessively, often by using bacteria-laden water. She may not be able to read the instructions for sterilizing.

The result is the preventable destruction of small children, mainly because of unfortunate advertising promotions. James Grant, the executive director of UNICEF, estimates that ten million children suffer—and as many as one million die each year—from malnutrition and other diseases associated with inadequate breast-feeding and the use of breastfeeding substitutes.

Over the years, many American and European mothers have tried to help by boycotting the products of companies like Nestlé (including Beech-Nut baby foods, since Beech-Nut is a subsidiary of Nestlé). The *Harvard Business Review* discussed the boycott as one example of the ways consumers and investors attempt to push corporations toward ethical behavior. The *Review* says that although the numbers of "ethical" consumers and investors are small, their effects are sometimes large. By 1982, it seemed that Nestlé was about to respond at last.

Now, the World Health Organization and UNICEF have passed an international code asking for restrictions on the marketing of infant formula. Compliance with the code is voluntary, but presumably many of the 155 countries that voted for the code will pass enabling legislation. Only one country voted against the code: the United States, where three corporations (Bristol-Myers Company, American Home Products, and Abbott Laboratories) control a $2 billion industry in the manufacture of formula.

Now there are questions, too, about some U.S. formula brands. This time it is not the advertising push in question so much as the safety of the formula products themselves.

The history of formula manufacture resembles the history of commercial baby foods, except that, to their honor, formula companies seem to have been more responsible in solving their nutritional problems.

About thirty years ago, for instance, one manufacturer initiated a process of sterilizing formula at temperatures that turned out to be high enough to destroy vitamin B_6.

As a result, the babies who were fed the formula suddenly came down with a variety of distressing symptoms, including muscle twitching and convulsions. The manufacturer moved quickly to restore vitamin B_6, and the problem was solved.

Recently, two brands of formula from Syntex Laboratories were found to be defective because they lacked essential chloride. The babies affected numbered between 20,000 and 50,000. They were allergic to milk, and had been fed only these soy-based brands of formula, Neo-Mull-Soy and Cho-Free, for long periods of time.

No baby died, but many of them became seriously ill from chloride starvation (hypochloremic metabolic alkalosis). Some of the infants suffered drastic weight loss. Some developed very slowly. One mother, for instance, reported a soy-fed child who, at nineteen months, could still not sit up. The fear is that these babies may suffer long-term learning disabilities, and they may need special education.

Two Washington-area couples, Alan and Carol Laskin and Lynne and Larry Pilot, formed a group called "Formula" to publicize the problem and to keep track of the babies affected. The "Formula" group sends out a questionnaire for parents from Box 39051, Washington, DC 20016, without charge, as a way to help analyze potential problems. Findings from the questionnaire go to the Center for Disease Control in Atlanta.

Both the Center for Disease Control and the National Institutes of Health have been cooperating in the parents' project. And Syntex Laboratories have redesigned the products.

One result, too, is that the U.S. Food and Drug Administration has asked for stiffer controls on formula manufacture. By 1981, Congress was considering a bill to establish quality control for infant formula. The bill requires better record-keeping, and it provides for speedy recall in the event of problems.

So formula may be better guarded now than it has been in the past, or at least there ought to be quick legal recourse. Unfortunately, these tight controls may also inflate formula prices dramatically.

Meanwhile, mother's milk continues to be worth the mother's time and worth whatever troubles she may encounter.

Breastfeeding can be difficult. But a mother can breastfeed even if she works at other jobs besides taking care of her baby. Hard-working mothers in Israel and the USSR manage it—with considerably more help from their employers than American mothers usually receive.

You may be surprised to learn that mothers of twins and even mothers of triplets breastfeed in about the same percentages as the mothers of one-at-a-time children. Liberated women seem to nurse as enthusiastically as the more conservative old-fashioned mothers. Mothers of hospitalized babies have been able to nurse, as have mothers who are themselves handicapped. Even adoptive and foster mothers have been able to nurse.

HELP WITH BREASTFEEDING

You can get help.

La Leche League is an international organization devoted to helping mothers to nurse their babies. A group of experienced and charitable mothers began the organization in 1956 to help other women. La Leche is Spanish for "the milk," from a shrine in St. Augustine, Florida, dedicated to "Nuestra Señora de la Leche y Buen Parto," or "Our Lady of Plentiful Milk and Happy Delivery." Now La Leche League has chapters across the world and in virtually every U.S. city. You can participate in discussions with other mothers and benefit from the encouragement of a group with similar interests and, most likely, similar problems.

Or you can get in touch with a La Leche League leader who is an expert on coping with all the usual and unusual problems of breastfeeding. For instance, she can often tell you what medications are safe for a nursing mother and she knows something about breast infections, sore nipples, family stress.

Your doctor and hospital will probably have information about La Leche League chapters and about the other support groups that help nursing mothers in each locality. Or get in touch with La Leche League International at Franklin Park, IL 60131. La Leche League publishes The Womanly Art of Breastfeeding, the standard manual for the nursing mother. Another book, long and detailed, is Dorothy Patricia Brewster's You Can Breastfeed Your Baby . . . Even in Special Situations. The special situations cover every imaginable problem from nursing a retarded, defective, or seriously ill infant to bringing back milk for an older baby.

Remember that nine out of ten women can nurse their babies without difficulty. The problems are usually ones with quick solutions. The only times when a mother definitely should not nurse is when she suffers from active tuberculosis, typhoid fever, or malaria.

The best time to start preparing for breastfeeding is during pregnancy. Don't use soap on your nipples either during pregnancy or after the baby is born. Warm water will clean them well enough. Cracked dry skin can create misery for a nursing mother, and soap causes more drying than you'd want to risk.

Some mothers also use hydrous lanolin on their nipples every day during the last months of pregnancy. In those last months, massage your nipples gently and, during your bath, try using your fingers to express some colostrum.

It is wise to toughen up the nipples—but in a gentle way. Any massage or pulling that hurts is doing more harm than good.

Your nipples may be flat, or they may be inverted so that they turn inward when you try to pull them out. If so, the ends have never been exposed to air. They are tender, and when the nursing baby pulls on them, they can get painful. In the first days after birth, also, a new mother's breasts sometimes swell with milk and the other fluids involved in getting the milk started. The breasts can be large and hard at first, and if the nipples are flat, it's like asking the baby to nurse a basketball. It's frustrating, to say the least.

If your nipples do seem tender or flat during pregnancy, try wearing a nursing bra with the flaps open so that your clothing rubs gently against the nipples.Or you can wear hollow plastic breast shields designed to create a light, unnoticeable suction that pulls the nipple out little by little.

When the baby is born, nurse as early and as often as you can. Many mothers nurse the baby right after delivery. The nursing reassures the baby about this new world, and it is a thrill to the mother and father.

But don't worry if the baby doesn't nurse right away. A newborn baby may be too exhausted or too sleepy or, once in a while, too agitated to nurse. The natural instincts will come along in time.

Once nursing is established, nurse as long as you can. Nurse on one breast for ten minutes or so, and then switch to the other side for a long nursing. Reverse the order next time.

Don't believe the every-four-hours convention of baby feeding.

Successful breastfeeding depends upon frequency and length of nursing. As babies nurse, they are guaranteeing their milk supply. They are bringing in milk. You may get the impression in the first few weeks that your baby intends to bring in enough milk for triplets. The baby is just intending to be a survivor.

In fact, newborn human beings were probably meant to be

almost continual feeders. Doctor-scientists Marshall Klaus and John H. Kennell of Case Western Reserve University report a correlation between the protein content of milk in each animal species and the frequency of nursing for that species. As the protein of an animal's milk decreases, the young of that species must nurse more often. Since the protein content of human milk is naturally low, the baby just starting out has to nurse almost constantly. Nature meant it that way.

Stick with it. It will get better. Engorgement and sore nipples improve within days. After a few days, the let-down reflex operates only when you need it. The baby slowly learns to adapt to the mother's biological clock.

Before long, you will be back to feeling like your normal self. And the baby will be sleeping for tolerably long periods of time.

Sometimes you just need to get through one more tough night, and then in the day everything will begin to look bright, and you won't have to send out for bottles after all. Sometimes even just a long hot bath will be enough to relieve discomfort.

Breast size has nothing to do with nursing ability. A woman with small breasts can make copious milk.

But some women with large breasts are particularly uncomfortable when they first start nursing, and they need the help of a support bra. Even in the era of braless fashions, it is wise to own—and wear—a good nursing bra. A nursing bra may be more comfortable in the last months of pregnancy, and just after the baby is born, you may want to wear it at night, too.

Be careful to have a thoroughly comfortable place to nurse, with pillows and armrests at the right angles. If the breasts are uncomfortably heavy at first, you don't want to add other sources of muscle fatigue or soreness.

Fold handkerchiefs or nursing pads inside your bra to guard against milk leakage during the first few days of nursing. Soon you will have exactly the right amount of milk for your baby, and leakage won't be a problem, but especially with a first baby, Mother Nature is sometimes overenthusiastic. Just don't use anything plastic. Remember how those old plastic raincoats used to feel?

Notice that we are nowhere recommending more than a rare supplement of formula. Breastfeeding is like few other enterprises in the great cruel world: You get out of it exactly what you put into it. Babies produce milk in exact proportion to their needs, and they bring it in by the length of time and the energy they spend nursing. If you use a formula supplement, it will cut down on the baby's nursing time and keep your milk supply from building up.

Also, feeding only breast milk for the first few months helps prevent your baby from developing allergies.

If a mother has been ill and the baby is not gaining, she might then use a formula supplement for a short time. But the best way to build up the milk supply is by repeated nursing. And, of course, the mother should drink plenty of milk herself and eat nourishing foods.

Insofar as possible, the nursing mother should avoid medication that is not essential. As a matter of policy, she definitely ought to avoid "optional" medication, and we include aspirin, barbiturates, bromides, iodine, and extraordinary dosages of vitamins. Get your doctor to check the literature on prescribed medicine to be sure the medication will not create problems, or get in touch with La Leche League for information.

You will probably want to have an emergency bottle or two on hand. If you are serious about breastfeeding, however, it is not worth your while to buy any complicated set of disposable linings, bottle warmers, or sterilizer. A bottle can be sterilized in an ordinary saucepan.

When a mother must be away from her baby for several hours a day, she may need to go to some trouble to keep her milk supply stimulated. The easiest way is to express some milk by hand every few hours. The milk can be kept refrigerated in a sterilized bottle for up to two days. A baby-sitter or a hospital can use it to feed a baby mother's milk by bottle.

Hand expressing takes some practice, and it's a nuisance, of course. The amount of milk can be meager at first. But the routine can be made to work. Many mothers are able to provide milk for a hospitalized baby and to resume nursing when the baby comes home.

Especially if the baby is more than a few months old, the mother can return to an eight-hour-a-day job and still feed the baby on mother's milk. At one high school, three teachers meet for the purpose every noon in the ladies' lounge. Regular hand expressing takes a lot of energy and careful planning, but it can be done.

An inexpensive hand pump can also be useful, especially when the mother has not yet learned hand expression. But the hand pump can be uncomfortable at first.

A hospital-style electric pump would be appropriate for the mother who needs to create milk artificially over a long period of time. Naturally, it would be preferable for a mother to visit the hospital to nurse her baby. But that is not possible for a premature or a very ill baby who is unable to suckle normally. These electric pumps may be rented in many areas, and the cost may even be covered by medical insurance.

If you are away at your job all day, consider having the baby brought to you. Perhaps the baby-sitter could bring the baby at noontime. Some socially responsible companies arrange for child care on the premises—and, yes, they do report that they have lower turnover and happier employees. Some of their employees could make more money elsewhere, but they want to stay where their children are welcome.

Many women are able to make special arrangements. A well-known television personality nurses her baby in the limousine on the way to work. She works with a nanny backstage and had a nursery set up for the baby. On humbler levels, one baby we know sits in an infant seat looking at the world through the front window of a music store. And her mother, the store manager, is right there with her.

Mary Shelley wrote her famous novel, *Frankenstein*, while nursing her baby and leaning over him to her desk. Her baby's name was William, and you can notice to your horror that, in the novel, the monster's first victim is a charming baby boy—named William.

We don't all have limousines or even music-store windows. But breastfed babies are especially portable. They tend to remain cheerful, and they don't have to be accompanied by a lot of paraphernalia. Just stick an extra diaper in your pocket and bundle the baby on your arm or your back.

Of course, taking your baby to some jobs may be impossible. If you must return to work immediately after the birth of your baby, at least plan to breastfeed for whatever period you can, however short. You can do an immense amount of good with only a few weeks, days, or even hours of breastfeeding.

The ideal time to breastfeed, if you can possibly manage it, is up to two or two and a half years, or up to the time when all the baby teeth have come through. Of course, by that time, the baby also ought to be eating a balanced diet of table foods. And the older baby would not be nursing so often as to preclude outside commitments.

Prolonged nursing is unusual in our society, but it seems to be what nature intended. More women breastfeed for a longer time than you might think. They just may not be talking about it outside of support groups like La Leche League.

In any case, the best weaning is done by the baby. The growing baby gradually forgets about nursing, without any feeling of loss or distress. A toddler gets too busy to lie around drinking milk.

Any weaning that must be done before the child reaches that stage of natural forgetfulness ought to be done slowly, gradually, and with love. Begin nursing the baby, and then sneak in the bottle nipple with body-temperature milk in it. It might even help to bring in the bottle from under one's clothing.

Leave off nursing gradually for your own comfort as well as the baby's. An abrupt weaning can be very painful to the mother, and if she were ill, it might be better for her to contrive to keep on nursing than to combine her illness with the additional stress of an abrupt weaning.

BOTTLE-FEEDING

If the time comes when you must turn to commercial formula, here are some ways to make bottle-feeding as natural as possible.

Choose a formula with your doctor's advice. The American Academy of Pediatrics recommends a proprietary formula containing iron and vitamins for babies who cannot be breastfed. And the Academy recommends using formula for the whole year.

As you choose a formula, beware of labeling phrases like "Contains only the most desirable features of mother's milk." That may be a euphemism meaning that a few natural ingredients have been skipped over.

Proprietary formula is ordinarily based on cow's milk. When babies are allergic to the cow's-milk base, a pediatrician may recommend a soybean- or a meat-based formula. Occasionally, goat's-milk formula may be used when nothing else agrees with the baby, but it is not adequate in itself because it lacks the essential vitamin B_{12}, which must be given as a supplement.

Commercial formula is ordinarily available in three forms:

First, ready-to-feed formula is already mixed with water. You can buy it in 32-ounce cans ready to be poured into your own bottles. Or you can buy disposable nursing bottles in 4-ounce, 6-ounce, or 8-ounce sizes.

As you might suspect, ready-to-feed formula is by far the most expensive, and it is wasteful. It might be the formula of choice, however, if your water supply were polluted, if the water were high in salt or nitrates, or in situations where you cannot guarantee cleanliness.

Second, liquid concentrate formula is meant to be diluted with an equal amount of water.

Third, powdered formula is prepared by mixing 1 level tablespoon of powder with 2 ounces of water. Naturally, powdered formula is the least expensive form.

Always be sure to dilute formula exactly according to the directions. Undiluted formula concentrate can be dangerous, and overly diluted formula will not provide enough calories.

Never supplement a formula with powdered or dry milk. Too great a concentration of cow's milk, in whatever form, can overload a baby's immature kidneys and dangerously increase the solids in the blood.

Also, never supplement a formula with honey. In rare instances, honey can cause botulism in babies, but in any case, it is an unnecessary sweetener. The formula will taste just as good to the baby without sweetening, and the baby will take it just as well one way or the other.

In an emergency, you can prepare formula at home by the following recipe. Notice that the base is evaporated milk, which is produced by removing a little over half the water from fresh milk, and then adding vitamin D and sometimes vitamin A.

Make sure to distinguish evaporated milk from condensed milk, which is produced by removing about two thirds of the water from fresh milk and adding a considerable amount of sugar, with no vitamin fortification. Condensed milk of this sort is suitable for making fudge. Evaporated milk is fine for making yogurt or for reconstituting whole milk, and it has a reasonably soft and digestible curd.

EMERGENCY MILK-BASED
INFANT FORMULA

1 13-ounce (390 ml.) can
  vitamin-fortified evaporated milk
2 tablespoons (30 ml.) light corn
  syrup
18 ounces (540 ml.) boiled water

Blend the evaporated milk, corn syrup, and boiled water thoroughly. Pour into sterilized bottles. Keep refrigerated. Warm to body temperature before feedings.

Of course, you should resume normal feedings of mother's milk or proprietary formula as soon as possible. Babies fed homemade formula need supplements of vitamins A and C and, as they grow, iron.

When you shop for bottles, keep in mind what a human nipple looks like and choose bottle nipples that are short, flat, and fairly flexible, with rounded edges. Brands like Nuk-Sauger or Playtex Nursers come with naturally shaped nipples. These plastic nursers take sterile disposable liners into which one pours the formula. The liners look rather like long sandwich bags, but they are convenient and require no sterilization.

The long pointed nipples of old-fashioned bottles are not appropriate for a baby under four months old. In addition, the traditional glass bottles often require purchase of a large sterilizer, and parents may feel like Pierre and Marie Curie when they get into the job of sterilizing.

Here is how to sterilize bottles, nipples, baby silverware, or medicine droppers by the aseptic method.

Step 1. Wash all the implements thoroughly, including any spoons or dishes you intend to use in preparing the formula.

Step 2. Place the implements in a pan of water. A baby-bottle sterilizer will have a rack to hold the bottles and keep them from clanking together.

Step 3. Slowly heat the water to boiling, and boil for 5 minutes. Let cool to room temperature before uncovering.

Step 4. Lift the implements out with sterilized tongs. Place on a rack or a clean towel and let them air dry before preparing and adding the formula. Refrigerate formula with the nipple covered.

The terminal method of sterilization is appropriate to prepare a two-day supply of formula.

Step 1. Prepare formula and pour the proper amount into each of a day or two-day supply of clean nursing bottles. Screw nipples and caps loosely into place.

Step 2. Place the bottles in a deep sterilizer, either on a wire rack or towel folded in the bottom of the sterilizer. Add 3 inches of water to the sterilizer, and place on stove to heat.

Step 3. When the water has come to a boil, cover and keep at a rolling boil for 25 minutes. At the end of that time, remove from the heat and leave covered until cool enough to touch. Cooling too quickly may cause a film to form on the top of the formula. This film could clog the nipples during feeding.

Step 4. Tighten caps and store the bottles in the refrigerator. Sterilized formula should be used within 48 hours.

Unbreakable plastic bottles can be sterilized in boiling water as well as glass. Keep plastic bottles from smelling sour by soaking them in a solution of water and baking soda. Then rinse them thoroughly.

Do not use a microwave oven to sterilize. Use for heating as long as there is no metal bottle cap.

A few physical and psychological safeguards are essential to bottle-feeding:

- You can buy bottled water for preparing formula, but before you do, satisfy yourself that it is more sterile and less polluted than your own boiled tap water would be. Many bottled waters are sold only for their superior taste and not for their sterility.
- Always warm formula to body temperature. Don't fail to test some drops on your wrist before you offer it to the baby.
- Be sure the formula comes from the nipple drop by drop so the baby will not get it too fast. A small baby can choke easily. It is important to satisfy a baby's sucking instincts with a long, slow feeding; bottle-feeding ought to take at least 20 minutes, just as nursing would.

Failure to satisfy the sucking instinct may cause the baby distress at the time. It may also bring on habits of tongue-thrusting (necessary to keep from choking on free-flowing formula) or finger- and thumb-sucking, which may, in turn, cause dental and orthodontic problems in the future.

Probably, the flat, naturally shaped brands of nipples will flow slowly enough. Or you can buy "blind" nipples with no holes in them and then punch your own miniature holes.

Do not keep any nipple that allows the formula to flow freely, instead of drop by drop.

- As you feed the baby, make sure the formula fills the nipples and the neck of the bottle, without air bubbles.
- Hold the baby on alternate sides for each feeding, just as you would have to if you were nursing. You will be helping the baby's eyes to coordinate and to develop correctly.
- Do not let the baby lie absolutely flat while bottle-feeding. None of us could drink well if we were flat on our backs. Besides the risk of choking, a flat position allows the formula to stay too long in the baby's mouth. Formula pooling in the back of the baby's throat could lead to ear infections.
- It is never safe to prop the bedtime bottle in bed. If a baby takes a going-to-sleep bottle in bed, the formula may ferment in the baby's mouth all night long. Formula and juice given at night in this way are a major cause of tooth decay in small children. And, of course, night-long sucking on an artificial nipple is not conducive to correct development of the mouth and teeth.

33

If you are ever tempted to prop a bottle as a pacifier, at least put only plain sterile water in it.

- Clean the first baby teeth after each bottle-feeding by rubbing them with a piece of gauze.
- Hold your baby close for every feeding. The baby ought to see a loved human face along with the nourishment. It's an emotional occasion for the baby, and you ought to have the privilege of being connected with it.

Milk is the baby's survival. But it is also the baby's first social life. As, within hours of birth, a baby learns to love milk, so the child learns within weeks to love the parents who bring the milk.

As months go on, the baby typically tries to reach out to give those loved parents some food. Your baby hands you a soggy cookie, or attempts to put the spoon into your mouth.

Then you know you've won. It's an infant thank-you. It's the first reciprocal gesture. It's the rest of the life ceremony that you began with the first nursing.

Your child has come around to knowing who you are and why you're there.

CHAPTER THREE

GOOD FOOD FROM THE BEGINNING

Dan Gerber started his company because he found the labor of making baby food at home just too exhausting. Or so says a Gerber Products publication called "The Story of an Idea."

Picture Mr. Gerber back in 1927. He is spooning peas directly out of a can. And with his spoon, he tries to push the peas through a small strainer. An infant daughter is waiting impatiently for her cold, canned peas. Perhaps the scene didn't really go according to the illustration in the booklet, but Gerber Products does have a way of making home cooking sound strenuous for the parents and unappetizing for the child.

Actually, many baby foods call for nothing more complicated than a couple of minutes with a fork. And, without much in the way of work, you can do a lot better than canned peas pushed through a strainer.

One reason that making your own baby food is not all that difficult is that a baby who is old enough for something besides milk is also able to chew a bit. The big-enough baby does not need perfectly smooth, processed, liquefied foods.

How old is old enough?

The American Academy of Pediatrics recommends that parents wait until babies are four to six months of age before they start solid foods.

In the past, these times have tended to go by fads. For some years, the trend was toward earlier and earlier solids, so that people joked about getting out three kinds of cereal on the delivery table. Mothers seemed to race to see who could manage to stuff the greatest variety of prepared baby foods into their babies at the earliest possible time.

In its annual report, Gerber Products says those days are returning. But the remark may be just wishful thinking. Now medical authorities are nearly unanimous in agreeing with the American Academy of Pediatrics. It's a rare physician who will want to start solids before four months. Physiologically, an infant's digestive system is not ready to use any food but mother's milk or formula for at least three months. At best, food given too early might pass through undigested. Many a mother who fed a tiny infant spinach or beets has received nothing but a green or red diaper for her pains. At worst, the early food causes allergies, rashes, or digestive troubles, or in a rare case, methemoglobinemia. A very young baby may react badly to a new food, but if you begin the same food several months later, there will be no sign of trouble.

Normally, before a baby is born, the infant liver stores iron enough to last for up to six months or more of an all-milk diet. If the baby is born at full term and if the mother is in good health and is herself well nourished, there is not likely to be any problem about adequate iron or vitamins.

Since human milk contains a form of iron that the body absorbs rapidly, the baby who is entirely breastfed will get enough iron naturally for some months. Mother's milk from a well-nourished woman also contains an adequate level of vitamins and minerals.

Remember, too, that if a nursing mother is taking supplementary vitamins herself, some will show up in the milk.

Proprietary formula is already fortified with vitamins and minerals for the bottle-fed baby, and the American Academy of Pediatrics recommends that, when commercial formula is used, it be one that contains iron suitable for an infant.

So, generally, extra vitamin and iron drops are not desirable for a baby under six months old. There are exceptions:

- When the baby is premature, so that its body did not have the opportunity to store iron in the last weeks before birth
- When the nursing mother is ill or has a history of poor nutrition
- When the baby is fed homemade formula or another type of formula that lacks iron and vitamin C

- When the baby has a medical problem that indicates a need for caution about iron in the diet

Some doctors prescribe vitamin drops very early just as a precaution. Or when solids are delayed past the mid-year point, the pediatrician will probably want to add vitamin and iron supplements.

Unless the pediatrician specifically recommends something else, the vitamin supplements appropriate for a small infant are vitamins A, C, and D.

B-complex vitamins are present in milk and in many other foods, and in any case, it is possible that too much of the B vitamins too early can predispose a very young baby to allergies.

Most forms of milk—fresh milk, dry or canned milk, infant formula—are fortified with vitamin D. And most older babies will be getting vitamin C in juices and in fruits and vegetables.

Before six months of age, then, most babies are well supplied with 100 percent adequate nourishment from their mother's milk and even from a commercial formula that substitutes for mother's milk. They don't need much else.

You could wait even longer than six months to begin other foods. Dr. John H. Kennel, co-author of *Maternal–Infant Bonding*, has stated that breastfed babies of well-nourished mothers can survive quite well without solids for up to one year. Dr. Myron Wynick, pediatrician and nutrition expert at Columbia University, believes that a totally breastfed baby might grow especially slowly after six months.

But otherwise, the doctors do not see any risk in delaying solids into the second half of the first year. There may, however, be risks related to failure to take advantage of the right time in the baby's psychological development.

Your baby is instinctively likely to know just the right time to begin. Most babies want to eat solid foods by the time they are six or seven months old. By that age, they possess a tooth or two. It's a critical period for a baby to learn to chew, and by then you can see how obviously and enthusiastically the baby wants to learn about chewing and biting. Delay all solids much beyond seven months, and it is possible that the baby will have difficulty later in learning to chew and to swallow normally.

Mid-year babies react strongly to the scents of cooking. They are interested in the food on the table. Given the opportunity, they will grab food. They are quick to reach for brightly colored foods, but undoubtedly you will want to be more systematic about the introduction of new foods.

It is important to begin with foods that best supplement mother's milk or formula. These are the good sources of iron, protein, and carbohydrates.

It is also crucial to begin only one food at a time. Begin one food, and then if the baby has no bad reaction after four to seven days, you can introduce another type of food. You are safeguarding the baby's immature digestive system by allowing it to cope with just one food at a time.

Never introduce a new food if the baby is ill in any way. New foods should be avoided if the baby is suffering from diarrhea, cramps, or a rash.

Here is a sample schedule for starting first foods. It is only a sample. One of the best advantages of making your own baby foods is that you can cater to your child's specific physical needs and individual personality. We follow with specific recipes later in the book.

Week One

Breakfast: *Banana*

Mash up a bit of ripe banana with a fork, or put it through a food grinder. Bananas are bland and smooth, and they taste enough like milk that they won't surprise the baby too much.

Bananas are better nutrition than you might think at first; they contain potassium and a little iron, and provide vitamins A, B, and C.

Week Two

Breakfast: Banana
Dinner: *Cereal*

Cereal has long been the traditional first baby food. Cereal is desirable if your baby has a tendency toward diarrhea or if the weight gain is so slow that you feel that the baby needs extra calories.

Many parents claim that cereal at bedtime helps a baby sleep through the night. They use this as a reason to start cereal as early as two weeks after the baby is born. Yet how could anyone know whether cereal helps a baby to sleep? If it did not digest perfectly (certainly a possibility when it's given at an absurdly early age), it might have the opposite effect.

Begin with rice or barley cereals as wheat may cause allergies.

Use the recipes for cereals cooked from natural whole grains. Some adult cooked cereals are smooth enough for a baby. Others may need to be put through a grinder, a food processor, or blender (with liquid) after they are cooked. These include rice cereals, oatmeal, bulgur, and farina meant for adults.

If you use a commercial baby cereal, look for those that are:

- Enriched
- Iron-fortified
- Whole grain
- Unsweetened

Mix the cereal with a little mashed-up fruit, with mother's milk or milk formula, or with plain sterilized water. Later, you can use fruit juices or cow's milk.

Do not feed chunks of dry cereal to a baby under ten months of age; the pieces might cause choking.

Week Three

Breakfast: Banana
          Cereal
Dinner: Cereal
     Serving of meat, poultry, or vegetarian substitute

Use only fresh meat, and cook it thoroughly. Make sure that the meat is lean and that all the first meats or vegetables you give the baby are very well cooked and of a soft texture, without added salt.

Purée the meat or poultry with liquid. Until the baby is used to the different taste, mix it with mashed banana or with mother's milk or milk formula.

Do not add salt, butter, or lard.

Introduce a new meat each week, or, in the case of a vegetarian baby, a new vegetable or legume. Appropriate first meats or poultry are chicken, turkey, lean beef, iron-rich liver, and the organ meats that your family eats. Another alternative is simple unsalted beef broth. Avoid meats that are high in added nitrates or in natural fat. It is out of the question to offer a young child anything like bologna, bacon, frankfurters, salami, or smoked meats. If you have a choice, purchase meats that come from your own area of the country. The fresh, untraveled meats are less liable to come from medicated animals.

Week Four

Breakfast: Banana
           Cereal
Lunch: *Yellow vegetable*
Dinner: Cereal
           Serving of meat, poultry, or vegetarian substitute

Begin with a smooth, mild cooked vegetable, such as carrot or squash. Add vegetables one at a time about every four to seven days. Later, as the baby wants to chew more, you can introduce thin scrapings of raw carrot and other bits of raw green vegetables. Delay corn, cauliflower, and tomatoes.
Do not add salt or butter to baby vegetable dishes.
Of course, any unseasoned juice may be started at the same time as the vegetable from which it comes.
Babies often dislike vegetables at first because of the strong taste, so be sure to mix the vegetables well with mother's milk or milk formula or with a fruit or juice that the baby is ready for. In any case, you would likely be mixing the vegetable with water in order to get it to the correct consistency.
Be sure to see the recipe section on how to cook and soften vegetables thoroughly.

Week Five

Breakfast: Banana
           Cereal
Lunch: *Apple*
           Yellow vegetable
Dinner: Cereal
           Serving of meat, poultry, or vegetarian substitute

Scrape small shreds from a peeled apple. Or put thin apple slices through a food grinder. Or make unsweetened applesauce. Just quarter and core apples, and then cook them in water until they are tender. Then put them through a food mill. The peels will come off readily. Don't add any other flavorings or sweeteners to the baby's portion.

Week Six

Breakfast: *Fruit or juice*
           Cereal
Lunch: Apple
       Yellow vegetable
       Serving of meat, poultry, or vegetarian substitute
Dinner: Cereal
        Serving of meat, poultry, or vegetarian substitute
        Fruit or juice

Begin other new fruits, one at a time, about every four to seven days. Delay peaches for another month.

Of course, any unsweetened juice may be started at the same time as the fruit from which it comes.

Fresh-squeezed orange juice is expensive, but it is well worth the money for its natural vitamins. Water it down some for a baby, and be sure to strain out all seeds and pulp.

Week Seven

Breakfast: Fruit or juice
           Cereal
           Egg yolk, three times a week
Lunch: Fruit
       Serving of meat, poultry, or vegetarian substitute
       Vegetable
Dinner: Cereal
        Serving of meat, poultry, or vegetarian substitute
        Vegetable
        Fruit or juice

Eggs are one of the foods liable to cause allergy, especially the egg white. So it is wise to wait until past the baby's first birthday before you introduce egg whites. If your family suffers from allergies, you might also consider delaying the introduction of egg yolk until your baby is eight to nine months old.

To avoid developing allergy, hard-cook the yolk thoroughly, and start with very small amounts, ¼ to ½ teaspoon. Increase the amount gradually only if you see no sign of allergic reaction.

Remember that it will do no good to delay eggs if you give the baby egg-containing foods like custard, cookies, and breads.

Week Eight

Alternate meat servings with servings of *whitefish*.

Be sure to check local problems of fish contamination, and in any case to cook the fish thoroughly and watch the baby for any sign of allergic or digestive difficulties.

There are still reports of excessive mercury content in fresh tuna and swordfish, and at this point some Great Lakes fish are marginally unsafe with various contaminants.

Week Nine

Add *teething biscuits* and *whole-grain breads*, as the baby needs teething surfaces.

At this point, it is also time to allow other foods of rougher texture.

Home-baked breads taste better than commercial breads, and they can certainly be more nutritious. If you can get into the habit of making bread, you will find that the effort is not so great, especially when you consider the achievement in good eating for the whole family.

When you must purchase baked goods for the baby, avoid bleached flour and refined sugar.

Whole grains are satisfying to a baby whose urge to bite and chew is developing. But they can also be rich in iron and other nutrients, and they are a necessary complement to the vegetables and legumes of a vegetarian diet.

Some grains and starches add almost instant good taste and nutrition. For instance, sprinkle wheat germ on cereals and vegetables. You can also serve the baby chopped noodles or brown rice as a side dish.

About this time, add *smooth nut pastes*, such as peanut butter, and consider the other nutritious spreads, such as sesame seed paste.

A Sample Menu,
Eight to Twelve Months

Breakfast: Orange juice
　　　　　Egg yolk, three times a week (if no allergies)
　　　　　Cooked cereal (iron-rich, high-protein, unsweet-
　　　　　　ened), mixed with a mashed fruit or juice or with
　　　　　　mother's milk or milk formula
　Lunch: Serving of meat, poultry, whitefish, or a vegetarian
　　　　　substitute
　　　　　Fruit
　　　　　Vegetable
　　　　　Whole-grain bread or teething biscuit
　Dinner: Serving of meat, poultry, whitefish, or a vegetarian
　　　　　substitute
　　　　　Fruit
　　　　　Vegetable
　　　　　Whole-grain bread or teething biscuit

After one year, you are free to try cow's milk and other important foods.

One year may seem unusually late to begin cow's milk, but many doctors agree that's the way to avoid common milk allergies and digestive troubles. At twelve months, add fresh, whole or 2 percent milk, fortified with vitamin D. At about one year, too, a bottle-fed baby may be all right with milk rather than formula. But start gradually, with a few sips from a cup or with a partial bottle-full.

Milk carries excellent nutritional value. After one year, however, don't overrate the value of milk. As people grow older, milk is no longer a complete food.

At one year, you can also replace egg yolks with whole eggs.

You can add nutritious and important milk dishes such as cottage cheese and other mild cheeses, pudding, yogurt, and custard.

As the baby eats in ever more grown-up patterns, you can add more complicated, multi-ingredient foods, such as soups, stews, and baked goods. For instance, we recommend a fairly late intro-duction of tomatoes because of the common allergic reaction. But at the right time, tomatoes and tomato juice are a good source of vitamin C, and they are a favorite base for main dishes.

More quickly than you may imagine, your child will be eating a full range of superior foods. You will have, naturally and easily, worked your baby into a healthy pattern of eating that could last a lifetime.

A Sample Menu,
After One Year

Breakfast: Fruit or juice high in vitamin C
           Egg, three times a week
           Cereal or toast, unsweetened, with whole grains
           Milk

Lunch: Vegetable soup
           Serving or spread of meat, poultry, fish, cheese, seeds, or nuts
           Whole-grain bread
           Fruit
           Milk

Dinner: Raw vegetable salad
           Serving of meat, poultry, fish, or vegetarian substitute
           Cooked vegetable(s)
           Fruit
           Milk

Snacks: Fresh and dried fruit
           Raw vegetables
           Puddings, custards, and cheeses
           Whole-grain crackers and biscuits

CHAPTER FOUR
THE BEST FOODS FOR BABIES

THE BEST MEATS AND POULTRY FOR BABIES

Fresh or frozen meats are preferable
Lean and unsmoked, without added nitrates
Locally produced preferable

- Plain unsalted beef or chicken broth
- Calf liver and other organ meats, such as beef or pork liver, tongue, sweetbreads, kidney, heart, brains
- Chicken and turkey
- Lean beef and veal
- Lamb
- Fresh ham and low-fat cuts of pork, unsmoked and well cooked (until meat falls from bones and no hint of pink remains)

THE BEST FISH FOR BABIES

Fresh or frozen preferable, except for tuna and swordfish
Checked for uncontaminated sources, unpolluted waters

- Tuna and pilchard
- Whitefish: bass, catfish, cod, flounder, haddock, hake, halibut, lake trout, perch, pike, pickerel, pollock, snapper, sole
- Fatfish: herring, mackerel, salmon

- Shellfish: minced clams, lobster, oysters, scallops, shrimp, rarely crab (for older babies)

THE OTHER BEST MAIN DISHES FOR BABIES

- Legumes, vegetables, and whole-grains combined for a whole-protein vegetarian diet
- Cottage cheese and mild natural cheese rather than "cheese food," "cheese products," or "imitation cheeses"
- Egg yolk, scrambled, poached, or hard-cooked
- Whole egg after one year
- Tofu (soy curd)

THE BEST VEGETABLES FOR BABIES

Fresh and tender preferable
Peeled, scrubbed, and blanched, thoroughly cooked for babies under eighteen months old

- Asparagus
- Carrots, potatoes
- Kale, parsley, parsnips, Jerusalem (or root) artichoke, spinach, sweet pepper
- Sweet potatoes, yellow or winter squash, yams
- Green leafy vegetables

THE BEST LEGUMES FOR BABIES

Fresh preferable, as they are less gas-forming

- Peas
- String or waxed beans
- Kidney beans, lima beans, navy beans, and soybeans

THE OTHER BEST VEGETABLES
AND LEGUMES FOR BABIES
OVER ONE YEAR OLD

- Beets, broccoli, brussels sprouts
- Dried peas and beans
- Lentils
- Cauliflower, cabbage, kohlrabi, turnip
- Cooked celery
- Corn and onion in small quantities

THE BEST FRUITS FOR BABIES

Fresh, uncontaminated, washed and peeled

- Apples and pure applesauce
- Oranges
- Apricot, banana, blueberries, grapefruit, nectarine, pineapple, pears, peaches, prunes, pumpkin, tangerine
- Cantaloupe, honeydew melon, muskmelon

THE OTHER BEST FRUITS FOR
BABIES OVER ONE YEAR OLD

- Tomatoes
- Blackberries, raspberries, strawberries, with seeds strained out
- Currants, dates, figs, raisins
- Other dried fruits such as apple, apricot, peach, pear, prunes

THE BEST JUICES FOR BABIES

Fresh-squeezed preferable
Unsweetened and unsalted

- Orange
- Apple, apricot, grapefruit, pineapple
- Tomato, for babies over nine months old
- Vegetable blends, for babies over nine months old

THE BEST GRAINS AND
CEREALS FOR BABIES

- Barley
- Buckwheat
- Bulgur wheat
- Farina
- Hominy
- Millet
- Oats and oatmeal
- Brown rice
- Rye
- Whole wheat and wheat germ

THE BEST SPREADS AND
PASTES FOR BABIES

- Smooth peanut butter without hydrogenated oil, dextrose, sugar, or salt
- Smooth unsalted seed-and-nut pastes such as tahini (sesame seed paste)
- Fruit butters

THE BEST DESSERTS FOR BABIES

- Pure applesauce
- Fresh and dried fruits
- Yogurt unsweetened except with fresh or dried fruit, for babies over twelve months old
- Milk and fruit puddings, custards and junket, for babies over twelve months old
- Baked fruits, such as apples or bananas
- Fruit with nut paste or cheese

THE BEST SOURCES OF IRON

Cooking in an iron pan helps to add iron to foods

- Liver, heart, and other organ meats
- Meats and poultry
- Dried legumes

- Salad greens
- Wheat germ, whole wheat grains, and enriched cereals
- Egg yolk
- Nutritional (or brewer's) yeast
- Unsulfured blackstrap molasses
- Prunes and prune juice
- Apricots
- Raisins
- Bananas
- Potatoes

THE BEST SOURCES OF CALCIUM

- Milk and milk products
- Salad greens, except for beet greens and spinach (the oxalic acid binds calcium)
- Almonds
- Soy flour
- Clams, canned mackerel, canned salmon, sardines
- Unsulfured blackstrap molasses

CHAPTER FIVE

FINGER AND TEETHING FOODS

One advantage of making your own baby food is that you can create just the right textures for the condition of the baby's teeth and the strength of the baby's urge to chew. Go from puréed meats, for instance, to roughly grated meats to very tiny bits cut with a knife. Instead of applesauce, scrape shreds off raw apples with a spoon. Slice cheese in long strips. Let whole-grain bread dry in the air until it gets good and chewy.

Here is a list of foods that will feel good on those itchy, aching baby gums. The baby will love to hold them and play with them.

- Cooked carrots. For toddlers over eighteen months old, keep raw carrot sticks in a bowl of ice water in the refrigerator to hand out as instant snacks.
- Cooked beans
- Bananas
- Apple scrapes and slices, peeled for babies under eighteen months old
- Other raw, peeled fruits and vegetables (but not celery, which has strings that might choke a small child and that, if stored and served raw, may carry salmonella in the crevices)
- Strips of natural cheese
- Drained salmon and tuna chunks for babies over nine months old
- Strips of steak, chops, liver, for babies over twelve months old

- Chicken drumstick or other large piece, but with gristle or small bones removed, for babies over twelve months old
- Whole-grain bread cut into air-dried fingers
- Whole-grain teething biscuits and crackers (see our recipes)
- Hard-cooked egg slices, for babies over twelve months old
- Dried apricots or other dried fruits, raisins, currants, figs, for babies over twelve months old
- Shreds of lettuce, for babies over nine months old
- Chopped noodles and other enriched pastas and brown rice
- Seedless raw cantaloupe, honeydew melon, muskmelon, nectarines, tangerines, pineapple chunks (but remove the tough membranes, especially on tangerines and nectarines), for babies over twelve months old

CHAPTER SIX

UNSAFE FOODS

Mothers always worry, quite rightly, about babies choking on teething and finger foods. The best way to prevent that is always to stay near a baby who is eating. Don't let a baby run around holding hard foods (or other objects, for that matter).

Cook food, such as carrots and string beans, until you are sure that the baby is old enough to handle them raw, probably after eighteen months of age.

Do *not* give these small hard foods to any baby under a year old:

1. Raw celery—even for an older child, scrub the celery well and blanch it briefly in boiling water to get rid of the possible contamination of salmonella.
2. Raw peas and string beans
3. Nuts and peanuts
4. Whole corn kernels
5. Popcorn
6. Whole or unseeded berries
7. Dry cereal
8. Hard candies
9. Potato chips

CHAPTER SEVEN

HOW TO AVOID JUNK FOOD AND MAKE ORDINARY FOOD MORE NUTRITIOUS

The favorite treat foods for children these days are just about 100 percent junk. Reward children with lollipops, ice cream cones, soft drinks, potato chips, hot dogs—and you are going along with the rest of the world toward making your children into "junk-food junkies."

Each season presents its special temptations toward the unnatural. At some point, your big children will be out for Halloween. They'll be attending birthday parties. Santa Claus will be handing out candy canes.

They will see the value that the rest of the world places on junk food. They will stand in line with you at drugstores where the candy is displayed right at a child's eye level by the cash register. Every time your children accompany you to the bank, to the department store, or even to the pediatrician's office, they will be offered lollipops or other goodies. A bank teller of our acquaintance once thrust a lollipop into the tiny fist of a three-month-old baby. The junk food seems to arrive into a child's hand at virtually every outing without any permission from the parents. It's a casual and irritating invasion, a junk-food army soliciting for its ruinous cause.

It's difficult to battle back when the opposing army all seem to be people of good will. Junk food is an unavoidable part of the usual neighborhood experiences of any American child.

Presumably, there comes a time when missing out would damage a child's psyche. You can't destroy a child's social life and ignore holidays in the name of good nutrition. Neither do you want to make junk food seem overwhelmingly attractive just because it is forbidden.

At least with a baby, you're starting fresh. The baby has no sweet tooth (not for refined sugar anyway) and no taste for salt. If a baby objects to a food, it is more likely because of uneven temperature or an unfamiliar texture than taste. Certainly, babies are not going to object to a mild sweet taste when milky sweet flavors are all they know.

As the baby food manufacturers are quick to point out, any sugars, salts, and spices in baby food are to please the parents and not the infant.

Adults may have the excuse of habit in their craving for sugars and salt. It's a kind of addiction. But there is no reason of any sort to give non-nutritional foods to a baby. The baby is not in the habit of self-destructive eating behavior.

Just exactly what is destructive about junk food?

First of all, junk food takes the place of superior foods. It pushes good food aside. And in place of good food, junk food gives empty calories.

That displacement is particularly evident in the diet of any child with a small appetite. The child can eat only so much, and if it's candy and cake, then it surely won't be vegetables.

REFINED SUGAR, THE ENEMY

The ubiquitous enemy in junk food is sugar. Not only is refined sugar the primary source of empty calories, it is also seductive. People quickly build up a taste for it, even an addiction. Adults knowingly and consciously ruin their waistlines and their teeth for it. Primitive peoples adopt sugar first of all the offerings of a supposedly advanced civilization.

In addition to its total lack of nutritive value, it appears that refined sugar is actively harmful in itself. Dr. Jean Mayer, the President of Tufts University and America's best-known nutritionist, has stated that there is nothing good he can say about sugar. Sugar, of course, is a major cause of tooth decay. And our unprecedented consumption of refined white sugar (sucrose) correlates with the increase in the rate of coronary heart disease and atherosclerosis (hardening of the arteries) in the United States. World-wide and historically, as the consumption of refined sugar has increased, heart disease has also increased.

Also, refined sugar requires little digestion since it is absorbed into the bloodstream very quickly. Insulin is then produced to metabolize the sugar. This causes the sugar level in the blood to drop, leaving an excess of insulin still circulating. The result is that the person desires more sugar to use up the excess insulin. And so the cycle goes on and on.

Many medical authorities feel that this cycle, disastrous to any idea of weight control, also may eventually lead to the development of diabetes in susceptible people.

Sugar has also been implicated in the behavior problems, hyperactivity, and learning difficulties of many children. Sugar is the first substance some pediatric allergists eliminate from the diets of their young patients.

The lure of sugar is such that Americans are not paying attention to its evils. Statistically, every man, woman, and child in the United States eats his or her own weight in sugar in every year. And people are eating more sugar all the time, by far the most of these sugars being the empty-calorie refined cane and beet sugars.

Suppose you were the absolutely average American, and you were increasing your consumption of sugar each year at precisely the national average. Do you know what would happen to you? You would be gaining more than nine pounds each and every year: You'd be getting fat.

Americans are getting fat. All the statistics have us getting no taller and much broader. This is the legacy we will give our children if we don't change our sugar-stuffed ways.

One problem is that many sugars are disguised in commercial foods that one would not sweeten in home-cooked versions. Canned soups, bouillons, broths, and vegetables are often sugared. Pineapple juice, already as sweet a substance as nature can produce, may have extra refined sugar added.

The foods that you might expect to be sweet are often sweet in unexpectedly high percentages. Children take in extraordinarily high amounts of refined sugar as they drink the traditional childhood beverages like Kool-Aid or eat the dry cereals marketed for children—even the supposedly "natural" cereals.

See our chart on the percentages of refined sugar in common

foods likely to be attractive to children or advertised for children. These percentages also reflect natural sugars—the sort you would find in oranges and apples, for instance—as well as the empty calories of refined sugars.

A relatively new method of disguising sugary ingredients in commercial foods is to list them under names other than sugar. Beware of overlooking empty-calorie sweeteners in foods when they are listed under varying terms.

These are the usual sugar additives in commercial foods:

- Brown sugar
- Brown sugar syrup
- Cane sugar
- Corn syrup
- Dextrose
- Fructose
- Glucose
- Honey
- Malted barley
- Maltose
- Molasses
- Sucrose
- Sugar
- Turbinado

None of these sugars holds any particular advantage over the others. Some, like honey and fructose, carry more calories per tablespoon, but, then again, they also carry more concentrated sweetening power so that one does not need to use them in the same quantity as other sugars.

A tablespoon of sucrose (ordinary refined table sugar), for instance, has 45 calories. The same amount of honey has 65 calories.

But you would need to use only about 30 or 35 calories' worth of honey to get the same sweetening power as provided by 45 calories of refined sugar.

The ideal, of course, is not to introduce refined sugar into any baby foods. But if the baby is to stay away from sugar for long, at some point the rest of the family will need to cut down on sugar, too.

AVOIDING SUGAR

Some reduction in sugar can be almost automatic. Begin with the honey or fructose substitute. Honey can replace sugar, and in half the amounts called for, in almost any recipe. The exception is jams and jellies, where you need a separate recipe in order to use honey successfully.

Be certain not to use raw honey in the first year of baby's foods, because honey sometimes carries botulism toxins in amounts that have affected infants.

Another step in reducing sugar is even simpler. Just make it a policy to use less sugar than is called for in any given recipe. Probably no one will know the difference. In some recipes, you can get away with no added sugar. Applesauce is better without extra sugar, especially if the apples are a naturally sweet-tasting variety.

When you use canned goods, look for a water pack—or else just wash off the sugar syrup.

Instead of refined table sugar, try some pleasant-tasting substitutes (mostly for people over one year old):

- Ripe mashed banana
- Extra vanilla
- Cinnamon or nutmeg
- Raisins
- Dried banana flakes or other dried fruits
- Orange juice
- Grated fresh fruit
- Applesauce

It goes without saying that you dare not use chemical sugar substitutes in baby food—or in any food meant for children. Any substance like saccharin or sorbitol could be dangerous to an immature system. And it is not wise for nursing mothers or pregnant women to drink the saccharin-filled diet soft drinks. The effects of small dosages of saccharin or sorbitol on a full-grown adult are debatable. Even for adults, though, the risks probably outweigh the benefits. Sorbitol can cause severe diarrhea, and saccharin may be a carcinogen. Certainly for small children, there is no conceivable benefit to such substances, only a risk that parents ought not to allow.

Don't let a baby develop a sweet tooth and, perhaps, the adult will not be tempted to sweeten foods at risk.

PERCENTAGE OF SUGAR IN SOME
FOODS MARKETED FOR CHILDREN
(Figures from the United States
Department of Agriculture)

	Total Sugars (percent)	Total Sucrose (Refined table sugar) (percent)
Kool-Aid, General Foods	95.58	same
Country Time Lemonade, General Mills	85.90	same
Sugar Smacks, Kellogg's	56.00	43.00
Apple Jacks, Kellogg's	54.60	54.00
Fruit Loops, Kellogg's	48.00	same
Raisin Bran, General Foods	48.00	11.00
Sugar Corn Pops, Kellogg's	46.00	39.00
Super Sugar Crisp, General Foods	46.00	36.00
Crazy Cow (choc.), General Mills	45.60	42.00
Corny Snaps, Kellogg's	45.50	45.00
Frankenberry, General Mills	43.70	38.00
Cookie Crisp (vanilla), Ralston-Purina	43.50	43.00
Cap'n Crunch, Quaker Oats	43.30	42.00
Cocoa Krispies, Kellogg's	43.00	41.00
Cocoa Pebbles, General Foods	42.60	42.00
Fruity Pebbles, General Foods	42.50	42.00
Lucky Charms, General Mills	42.20	42.00
Cookie Crisp (choc.), Ralston-Purina	41.00	40.00
Sugar Frosted Flakes, Kellogg's	41.00	39.00
Quisk, Quaker Oats	40.70	40.00
Count Chocula, General Mills	39.50	35.00
Alpha Bits, General Foods	38.00	same
Honey Comb, General Foods	37.20	37.00
Frosted Rice, Kellogg's	37.00	35.00
Trix, General Mills	35.90	33.00
Hostess Twinkies, Continental Baking	35.62	same

	Total Sugars (percent)	Total Sucrose (Refined table sugar) (percent)
Cocoa Puffs, General Mills	33.30	32.00
Zingers, Dolly Madison	32.32	same
Oreo's, Nabisco	32.17	same
Cracker Jacks, Borden	30.29	same
Raisin Bran, Kellogg's	29.00	11.00
C.W. Post (w/raisins), General Foods	29.00	18.00
C.W. Post (w/out raisins), General Foods	28.70	20.00
Frosted Mini Wheats, Kellogg's	26.00	same
Country Crisp, General Foods	22.00	18.00
Life (cinnamon), Quaker Oats	21.00	same
100% Bran, Nabisco	21.00	19.00
All Bran, Kellogg's	19.00	16.00
Fortified Oat Flakes, General Foods	18.50	18.00
Life, Quaker Oats	16.00	same
Team, Nabisco	14.10	12.00
40% Bran, General Foods	13.00	10.00
Grape Nuts Flakes, General Foods	13.30	7.00
Mountain Dew, Pepsico Inc.	12.66	same
Hawaiian Punch, RJR Foods	10.05	same
Total, General Mills	8.30	7.00
Wheaties, General Mills	8.20	7.00
Rice Krispies, Kellogg's	7.80	7.00
Pepsi, Pepsico Inc.	7.38	same
Ritz crackers, Nabisco	7.00	same
Grape Nuts, General Foods	7.00	0.00
Hi-C Grape, Coca-Cola Co.	6.21	same
Special K, Kellogg's	5.40	5.00
Corn Flakes, Kellogg's	5.30	3.00
Pop Tarts, Kellogg's	5.27	same
Coke, Coca-Cola Co.	5.27	same
Post Toasties, General Foods	5.00	3.00

	Total Sugars (percent)	Total Sucrose (Refined table sugar) (percent)
Kix, General Mills	4.80	4.00
Rice Chex, Ralston-Purina	4.40	4.00
7-Up, Seven Up Co.	4.14	same
Corn Chex, Ralston-Purina	4.00	same
Wheat Chex, Ralston-Purina	3.50	2.00
Cheerios, General Mills	3.00	same
Shredded Wheat, Nabisco	0.60	same
Puffed Wheat, Quaker Oats	0.50	same
Puffed Rice, Quaker Oats	0.10	same

THE PROBLEMS WITH SALT

It is also important not to encourage a taste for salt. The evidence is mounting that early emphasis on salt leads to a lifelong desire for salt. Overmuch salt has been associated with high blood pressure and hypertension in adults. And adults can have as much trouble giving up salty foods as they do in giving up the sugary forms of junk food.

Your baby will get the dietary minimum of essential salt without any additions. Sufficient salt (sodium) occurs naturally in milk, in many vegetables, and in meats, fish, and cheeses that are appropriate for small children. And a baby's kidneys are hard put to handle an overload of salt.

While parents might miss the taste of salt we have come to expect in a multitude of foods, a baby won't miss it. The baby will not eat better or find the taste better whether you add any salt or not.

AVOIDING SALT

You can take some steps to reduce the amount of salt the older people in your family may be used to. If you buy canned vegetables, look for those without salt. You can buy some foods without salt in natural foods stores: cheeses, peanut butter, mixed nuts, even several kinds of crunchy snacks similar to potato chips.

Do be sure to check the foods sold in natural foods stores for salt content. When other preservatives are removed, salt is sometimes put in, and it is liable to cause as much harm as the original preservatives.

Of course, salt is not the only seasoning that enhances flavors. A baby's food requires no seasonings, but for older people, experiment with other spices, such as bay leaf, garlic, onion, rosemary, and thyme as substitutes for salt.

The step-by-step method works in replacing inferior foods with superior nutrients.

FLOURS

Most of us are used to white flour, and whole-grain flours may seem too chewy or tough at first. Yet that chewiness is all to the good nutritionally. It's fiber, and fiber helps digestion. It's good for chewing, especially when a baby is just developing teeth and gum structures. Whole wheat flour retains the germ and the bran, and it also retains the original nutrients. Whole wheat flour is rich in ways white flour is poor, even when the white flour has been enriched. Enrichment replaces 4 out of 22 nutrients (iron, niacin, riboflavin, and thiamin). Those are an important 4, but they are not 22.

ENRICHING FLOUR

To get your family used to the more nutritious baked goods, begin by using enriched all-purpose flour that is unbleached. Unbleached flour retains more nutrients than the bleached varieties, and it has not been treated with chemical whitening agents. There is no difference in taste or in the texture of the finished product. The unbleached flour is slightly less white in appearance.

When you use a flour like cornmeal, look to see whether it is degerminated. Degerminated means that the germ, the center of the grain, has been removed. You don't want it removed because it's the best part. (But its presence makes the grain subject to spoiling. Germinated flour has a short shelf life and should be kept cool to guard it against rancidity.)

A number of flours, both white and whole wheat, are bromated. Bromates can cause skin reactions in susceptible people, so it is advisable to avoid bromated flours, particularly in baked goods that a baby will be eating. The word "bromated" will appear on the front of the package.

If you find that the available whole wheat flour is bromated, use graham flour, which is essentially the same thing.

The next step toward more nutritious baked goods is to use the "Cornell Triple-Rich Formula" without fail. The formula enriches any flour, whole or white, and it works in any recipe.

In the bottom of each cup of flour called for, add 1 tablespoon (15 ml.) soy flour, 1 tablespoon (15 ml.) powdered nonfat dry milk, and 1 teaspoon (5 ml.) wheat germ. Fill the rest of the cup with the flour you will be using in the recipe.

The Cornell formula adds calcium, iron, protein, and vitamins to baked goods without appreciably altering taste or texture. Because whole-grain flours are more nutritious than plain white flour, we use whole grains, along with the Cornell formula, in our baked goods recipes. But you can experiment with substitutions in almost any recipe.

Cake flour, for instance, is not ordinarily enriched, and it is nearly always bleached. But you can use ordinary white flour in a recipe that calls for cake flour, and then enrich it yourself. Before you sift the flour, just add the ingredients for the Cornell formula. And then for the light aspect of cake flour, also add 2 tablespoons (30 ml.) of cornstarch. Mix these ingredients. Then sift and measure the flour for the cake.

You can enrich other white flour recipes somewhat by mixing the white flour with one-third part whole wheat flour. The baked goods will still be as light and tender as those made with all white flour.

When you wish to use all whole wheat in a white flour recipe, substitute as follows:

- Finely milled whole wheat flour: cup for cup
- Coarsely grained whole wheat flour: ⅞ cup for 1 cup white flour

CEREALS

Quick-cooking or instant cereals have additives to decrease the cooking time. So do instant pudding mixes. If you cannot buy pure milled cereals or make your own puddings, at least buy the longer-cooking varieties. The preparation time is the same, and the extra cooking time is usually short.

Besides getting fewer additives, you will get more cereal for your money. Ordinarily, the quick-cooking cereal package will be the same price as the regular package, but it will weigh less.

You can add valuable enrichment to any cereal by adding a tablespoon per serving of nutritional (or brewer's) yeast, which is ordinarily sold in drugstores. A sprinkling of wheat germ can also be used.

THE CONTROVERSY OVER FATS

Among the vexing questions facing nutritionists these days is the one of cholesterol. How cholesterol levels relate to the increase in coronary heart disease, atherosclerosis (hardening of the arteries), and cancer of the breast and colon is a major area of disagreement.

We should remember that cholesterol is not unnatural. The human body synthesizes cholesterol. It is an essential substance that the body uses in the manufacture of sex hormones and bile acids, and of vitamin D as taken from sunshine. The acetate from which cholesterol is made is available from practically all foods. Although the cholesterol in foods is not well absorbed from the gastrointestinal tract, as more is taken in from food sources, less is manufactured by the body. Currently, the Food and Nutrition Board of the National Academy of Science National Research Council "makes no specific recommendations about dietary cholesterol for the healthy person." (That's the latest position, reported in "Toward Healthful Diets," *Nutrition Today*, May/June 1980, p. 10.)

The controversy goes on. The real culprit in the tendency of

American males to store up cholesterol and to develop coronary heart disease may be another factor altogether, and that is lack of exercise. Perhaps we don't need to cut down on saturated fats so much as we need to get out and get moving.

And fat may not be the only dietary problem to cause cholesterol build-up. A diet high in refined sugar may also raise the fat and cholesterol levels in the blood.

With the experts still uncertain, the safest way is to avoid refined sugar (we know that has no nutritional value for anyone) and to use the purest shortenings possible, a balance of both saturated and unsaturated fats.

Certainly, the experts do not disagree in one area. People who take in too many fats and oils of any kind will suffer one disease: obesity. As the most concentrated source of calories, fat in the diet makes fat Americans as surely as sugar makes fat Americans.

It is best to avoid getting a baby accustomed to fatty or greasy foods. The baby does not relish fat, refined sugar, or salt, and fortunately has no way of knowing that these are national eating addictions.

REDUCING FATS

Reducing fat in the diet means, essentially, reducing any kind of fat, saturated or unsaturated, animal or vegetable.

It means cutting out greasy junk foods, such as potato chips and pastries. It also may mean reducing the consumption of some foods that otherwise offer good nutrition: red meats, creams, butter and cooking oils, peanut butter, eggs, salad dressings.

You can begin painlessly by reducing the amount of fat or grease you use in cooking, using the cooking methods outlined in the next chapter. You can continue by reducing the amounts of red meat you use. Make your hamburgers a little smaller, your soups with more vegetables and less meat, your habits nearer those of a knowledgeable vegetarian. You can reduce meat automatically in many recipes for casseroles, meatballs, chili, international foods. And look for lean meats that are less marbled and that contain a lower percentage of fat than others.

Try mixing in a small amount of nutritional yeast, eggplant, or other nutritious nonfatty foods to replace some of the meat.

You can lower the fat content of butter while retaining its good taste by blending it with an equal part of hot water in a blender or food processor.

When you introduce your baby to cow's milk, consider using 2 percent milk as a substitute for whole milk which contains 3 to 3.5 percent fat. (Some percentage of fat is desirable in milk for small children, so don't begin with skim or nonfat milk until the baby is well into toddlerhood.)

FINDING "PURE" FATS

Insofar as possible, select "pure" fats. The choice is not easy. Many of the vegetable oils that are labeled as "pure" are not much better than the not-so-pure shortenings; the oils often contain the same preservatives. A high price does not necessarily indicate purity.

Dr. Ross Hume Hall, the biochemist, in his book *Food for Nought*, explains what happens to fats when they are processed. Processing changes the fatty acids, and no one has really identified the long-term effects of that change. Cold-pressed oils, butter, and lard melted at low temperatures are about the only fats which remain in their natural state throughout the processing. The other margarines, refined oils, and shortenings are all subject to refining methods which change their original character. Heating fats to high temperatures (as for frying) changes them.

One could use only nature's finest cold-pressed oils, pure butter, and lard, all of which are expensive. It is difficult to avoid processed fats. Pick the purest oils and select margarines which contain few unknowns. Many oils and shortenings contain questionable preservatives, such as butylated hydroxyanisole (BHA) and butylated hydroxytoluene (BHT). Labels that say "pure" or "natural" may be misleading, so be sure to read the fine print on the label. Shortenings may contain monoglycerides and diglycerides, fat derivatives which are used as emulsifiers. These particular additives seem innocuous, but some shortenings contain numerous other chemicals as well.

The idea, overall, is to control what goes into food by studying lists of ingredients, by making food yourself "from scratch," or by substituting superior foods whenever possible.

Obviously, it takes more than a little common sense to withstand the ridiculous pressures of advertising and the marketplace. You know that candy bars are not nutritious even when ads boast that some factories put in actual egg whites—and maybe even a little powdered milk. You know that dehydrated soup powders cannot possibly be as pure and as nutritious as homemade or even ordinary canned soups—despite advertising claims to the contrary.

KNOCKING OUT CAFFEINE

Caffeine, of course, is a drug. It is not appropriate for small children. You wouldn't put coffee in the baby's bottle, yet the ads for soft drinks and for cocoa suggest that they are all right for little children. Soft drinks contain almost as much caffeine as coffee or tea; cocoa contains even more.

Caffeine is a stimulant, and all the stronger a stimulant when it affects a child's small heart and lungs. Caffeine also stimulates high blood-sugar levels, which can then fall rapidly as the stimulant wears off. As many coffee-addicted adults know, it's a dizzying cycle of high blood sugar followed by sudden low blood sugar followed by the desire for more of the stimulant.

Caffeine stimulation is just about as debilitating as refined sugar stimulation. The roller-coaster effect is certainly not right for a child. All too many children get right into the caffeine cycle with soft drinks and cocoa before they are really past infancy.

AVOIDING CHOCOLATE

Baby food companies put out chocolate desserts for babies. Yet despite that commercial push, cocoa and chocolate are not good for children under two and should be seldom used after two. It goes without saying that chocolate is associated with highly sugared foods, as well as with caffeine. It can cause allergies so severe that a nursing mother would be wise to reduce her chocolate intake for fear of its causing an indirect allergy in her child.

ORGANIC FOOD CLAIMS

It is difficult to be sufficiently perceptive to avoid being tripped up by deceptive advertising claims and by outright fraud. Unhappily, the natural foods market is as tainted as any other. You cannot tell by a casual inspection whether vegetables and fruits are organic.

They may have been organically fertilized, or they may have been treated with every chemical spray going and look about the same, so natural-foods con artists can ask premium prices for the same old produce just by claiming that it is natural.

One clue is that some organic produce is not perfect and polished. It does not glow with artificial color. It may be smaller, and it is often less attractive than the heavily treated produce. If you see scars and blemishes, you're probably looking at the more nearly natural food.

About commercial products, we propose some guidelines to help differentiate natural and nutritious from unnatural and not-so-nutritious. Like all generalizations, these are not always true. But they come close:

- First, the longer the list of ingredients, the less likely that the food is natural or wholesome.
- Second, the more indecipherable the list of ingredients, the less likely it is you should eat them.
- Third, the more laughable the label's claims, the more likely there's a rip-off involved.

As Jean Mayer puts it, "Some commercial soft drink labels read like a qualitative analysis of the East River." It isn't only junk food ingredients that read like that. Think of the myriad products that claim to be "natural": unprocessed, unrefined, close to the farm, Mother Nature's own.

How about natural ice cream? Natural potato chips? Natural white bread? Natural candy? Natural beer?

Misspelled catch phrases on the label don't bring a food any closer to nature. The "All-Natural Hi-Proteen Energy Bar" is still a candy bar.

Of course, some non-natural processes are healthful and right. It is not wrong to make cheese out of milk, any more than it's wrong to make furniture out of wood, and most of us would prefer protection against mold and prevention of bacteria in all the right places. Some of the 5,000 food additives in regular use are downright nutritious. Ascorbic acid, for instance, is just vitamin C.

But the rip-offs come when bread made of bleached and unenriched white flour is labeled "natural" or when refined sugar remains the primary ingredient of supposedly "natural" cereals.

The Federal Trade Commission filed a complaint against Anheuser-Busch for "false, misleading and deceptive advertising" when the company claimed to sell "natural" beer.

Under rules proposed by the Federal Trade Commission, natural foods would:

- Undergo minimal processing after slaughter or harvest, only to make the food safe and edible, not to change its physical traits by cutting, grinding, pulping, or drying;
- Contain no artificial flavoring, color dyes, or preservatives;
- Contain no ingredients that fail to meet the first two standards;
- Not be falsely advertised as nutritious or safe simply on the grounds of being "natural."

The rip-offs in natural foods sales present one more reason to opt for home cooking where, to a considerable extent, you control the ingredients. Home-baked goods do not have to contain food colorings, and you choose the kind of flour. Homemade soup skips monosodium glutamate, modified starch, and high salt. Your salad dressing does not need vegetable gums for thickening.

If you can't live off your own farm, you probably can't avoid all the rip-offs. But when you cannot harvest and cook 100 percent from scratch at home, you can at least shop wisely and look for foods with ingredients that you've heard of and approve of.

CHAPTER EIGHT

GUIDELINES FOR THE COOK

How can you prepare baby food so that it is safe, clean, and nutritious? Some general rules apply, and we can guarantee that if you follow them, your homemade baby food will be superior to factory food in every way. You'll also discover that home cooking is not overly time-consuming.

CLEANLINESS

The first rule is to keep everything scrupulously clean, including the smallest spoon. Rinse dishes and utensils with boiling water. Wash your own hands thoroughly.

Don't forget to clean these items, too. They are easy to overlook, but they can carry contamination:

- The entire blender blade assembly
- The can opener
- The lids of cans, bottles, and jars
- The cutting board
- Knives, forks, and spoons while in use and any surfaces upon which they rest
- Storage containers and ice cube trays

Take care to keep food clean as you prepare it. Wash fruits and vegetables. Peel even those fruits and vegetables that you might not ordinarily peel for adult consumption.

Wash uncracked eggs before you use them. Never use any egg that has been the least bit cracked in storage. Do not add raw eggs

69

to milk or to any other uncooked beverage. Raw eggs are said to add nutritive value, but they can also add dangerous salmonella bacteria.

FOOD PREPARATION

Well done is always best done for baby. Cook foods completely for baby food, including meats, fish, and eggs.

You do not need expensive equipment in order to prepare good nutritious baby food. You can prepare many foods in the simplest way. Just mash banana, cooked carrots, cooked apples with a fork. A hand-operated food mill or grinder can purée vegetables and fruits, even without cooking. Or a hand-cranked food mill can grind most foods into suitably smooth textures, and it has the additional advantage of turning cooked apples into sauce without hours of peeling. A food mill is not heavy enough to purée meats successfully, but works on virtually anything else.

The "Happy Baby" food grinder, designed especially for baby food, costs about $5. The smaller of the two sizes can purée single servings beautifully. It's a good idea to carry one on trips as a quick and easy way to fix up one baby meal at a time.

An electric blender or food processor can be useful, although it is far from necessary. Its main use might be in blending fresh fruit and vegetable juices, which are far more nutritious and tastier than commercial juices.

The other advantage of a blender or food processor is that, with the addition of liquid, it can purée virtually any sort of food, even meats. If you use a blender or food processor skillfully, you can purée food to a precise texture, exactly according to the needs of an individual baby. You can't do that with a food grinder or mill.

Some blenders come with small blend-and-store jars. The jars attach directly onto the blade assembly of the machine, and then after the food is processed, you don't have to transfer it to a second container.

A blender or food processor can help to preserve nutrients because you can use it to purée raw foods before cooking them. This cuts cooking time and avoids pouring off the cooking water. Instead, the necessary liquid is blended in with the raw food; that liquid is important because it can dissolve vitamins from the food. It can be highly nutritious, and it ought not to be thrown away.

The one disadvantage of blenders or food processors is that they draw in air which can oxidize certain fragile B and C vitamins. Limiting blending time to short bursts will usually avoid this problem.

When you cannot use a blender, a food processor, or a food mill to purée raw, vitamin-packed foods, then employ cooking methods that avoid the necessity of draining off water.

For vegetables and fruits, use a steamer in an ordinary cooking pot. The steamer holds the food up away from the water, and the food cooks not in the water itself but in the steam from the water.

You can bake many vegetables and fruits, such as apples or bananas, without water. Or stir-fry your vegetables without water.

A pressure cooker or a slow cooker can also be a time-saving way to cook foods to a suitable degree of tenderness; these methods can help to preserve the vitamins in vegetables, soups, meats, and custards.

When you do have excess cooking liquid, figure out ways to reuse it. It's particularly good for softening baby foods or as a base for soups, broths, and stews. If you can, use it within 24 hours, otherwise freeze it in pop-out ice cube trays.

Of course, you can prepare the baby's meals directly from whatever foods you are preparing for the rest of the family. Just divide off a portion before anyone has added salt, sugar, spices, butter, or condiments. Then cook and purée that one portion until it is well done and tender.

Be especially careful also to remove bone, gristle, skin, and fat from a baby's portion of meat, poultry, or fish.

Some methods of cooking are especially conducive to good nutrition. These methods employ a minimum of grease, and they preserve a maximum of good nutrition:

- Oven roasting
- Oven broiling on a rack, with fat dripping off into pan
- Pan broiling with a vegetable spray lubricant rather than oil or grease
- Poaching, steaming, or baking
- Pot roasting or braising
- Browning meats by broiling on a rack rather than by pan-frying

Lecithin is a pure vegetable derivative that can be used in spray

71

form to coat pots and pans; it cuts down on the amount of grease you must use in cooking. It is even better to buy a liquid form from a natural food supplier and brush it on the pan.

For cooking and salads, use an unadulterated vegetable oil such as corn, olive, peanut, safflower, or sesame oil.

It might be well to note that using cast-iron cookware increases the iron content of foods. In fact, the changeover from iron to aluminum and stainless steel, according to Ernest Beutler in *Modern Nutrition in Health and Disease* (eds. Robert S. Goodhart and Maurice E. Shils, 1980) "has almost certainly had an adverse effect on dietary iron intake."

The rule for baby food is that meats must not be underdone, but vegetables and fruits must not be overdone. To overcook vegetables and fruits is to destroy nutrients as well as to destroy some of the good taste.

Vitamins and minerals are likely to be concentrated just under the skin, so pare fruits very thinly. When you cook fruits, cook them in their skins and then strain the fruits through a sieve or a food mill. Fruits and vegetables such as apples and carrots can be served to a child raw. Peel and then scrape them with the paring knife to yield paper-thin slices. Just be sure to wash them well.

And be careful to use fruits that are fully ripened (but not overripe). Certain unripe or overripe and unwashed fruit can bring on diarrhea in adults as well as children.

As soon as you have finished preparing any baby food, either use it or store it properly. Immediate refrigeration is especially important for any foods containing milk or eggs as bacteria grow rapidly in their rich nutritious media.

FREEZING AHEAD

If it seems convenient, you may want to make a routine of preparing baby food in advance. Fresh food is generally more nutritious, but in some situations, you may want to freeze or can your own baby food, especially if you need to prepare in quantity.

Most puréed baby foods, cooked or uncooked, can be frozen without problems. But there are a few exceptions. Bananas do not freeze well, nor do some sorts of custards and puddings. Combination dinners generally do fine in the freezer.

Try freezing baby food in meal-sized portions.

First, quick-freeze the food in pop out ice cube trays. After the food is frozen into convenient cubes, remove them from the trays, and keep the frozen cubes in labeled containers. Or, if you need to save space, put the frozen cubes into plastic bags.

Do not thaw and refreeze these cubes. Just remove what is needed at any one time. Reseal the rest and put it back in the freezer at once.

Do not let frozen baby food thaw even partially unless you are going to serve it within minutes.

Do not store baby food in the freezer for more than four weeks. It is a good idea to date the containers so that you can use the oldest ones first.

CANNING

Ordinarily, there would not be any practical reason to can large quantities of baby food at home. A baby needs specially puréed foods for only a matter of weeks. There is not much point in canning more than you need for those few weeks, and even less point in setting up a full-scale canning operation for small amounts of food. Only if you are already canning produce on a regular basis does it make sense to put up specially prepared baby food along with the usual canning.

Successful gardening, harvesting, and safe freezing and canning require some instruction. A good place to start is the agricultural extension service of the nearest land-grant university; you can also order instruction booklets from the Superintendent of Documents, U.S. Government Printing Office, Washington, DC 20402.

Only a few particular recommendations apply to canning baby foods. Of course, you will want to take maximum safety precautions whether you are canning for adults or for children. Even after processing in a pressure cooker, some meats and vegetables must still be boiled for 15 minutes, uncovered, before eating. Safety requires that you use standard glass canning jars rather than miscellaneous glass containers, such as leftover mayonnaise jars.

In canning or freezing baby food, avoid using a sugar syrup pack for the fruits. Some fruits, such as apples, can be packed in water, with the addition of ascorbic acid. (Ascorbic acid is nothing more than vitamin C, so it is not a harmful preservative.) Other fruits, such as blueberries, can be dry-packed.

If you wish to purée fruit prior to packing, simmer it until you can force it through a fine strainer or food mill. Then reheat and process according to the packing instructions. Sprinkle pears, peaches, and apples with lemon juice or ascorbic acid before canning to keep them from darkening, using 3 tablespoons (45 ml.) of lemon juice or ½ teaspoon (2 ml.) of ascorbic acid to a quart of water. Or add the ½ teaspoon (2 ml.) ascorbic acid to each quart of water-packed fruit before processing.

One canning preparation contains sugar, ascorbic acid, and silica aerogel (an additive used to absorb moisture). The pure ascorbic acid crystals are to be preferred, as they do not contain the sugar or the silica aerogel; they are also less expensive.

To make the pure crystals easier to use, you might want to add 9½ teaspoons (47 ml.) of fine sugar to each ½ teaspoon (2 ml.) of ascorbic acid crystals. Whirl the sugar in your blender first. Then stir thoroughly and add 1 teaspoon (5 ml.) to each pound of fruit to be canned or frozen. The sugar is not desirable, of course, but it comes to a minute amount added per serving, and it does make the packing go more smoothly. The one small jar of crystals is enough to pack about 100 pounds of fruit. And the crystals add vitamin C to the finished product.

SAFETY PRECAUTIONS

Remember that no sealed food is sterile from the moment the container is opened. Any food intended for a baby ought to be served soon after it is opened, long before it can start to spoil.

When you use any food from a jar, whether or not it is home canned, remove it from the jar before you heat it. Parents used to plunk the jars directly into a pan of hot water, and then spoon the food out to the baby right from the jar. As often as not, the same jar then went back into the refrigerator. This dangerous cycle guarantees the growth of spoiling bacteria.

Instead, remove the food from the jar, heat it thoroughly in something like the small cups of an egg poacher, and serve immediately. Once the food has been heated, plan to serve it, or else, if it goes uneaten, throw it away. Don't keep reheating the same baby food.

The chief cook for a baby needs to be vigilant, driving away dirt and preserving safe nutrients with unfailing enthusiasm. The safety of a small child is a basic and essential task. Any job that requires such constancy is by definition difficult, and the job is often rewarding only in negatives. You cannot catalogue the illnesses or troubles that do not occur. You can just be glad for a baby's good health and know that your vigilance as a parent had a lot to do with keeping that good health.

CHAPTER NINE

GOOD FOOD PSYCHOLOGY FROM THE BEGINNING

Each baby is an individual. Your baby combines the genetic heritage of both parents, and the intrauterine environment from conception has helped to shape your new little person. After birth your child continues to grow through the interaction of genetic potential and environmental influences.

Since nutrition is basic to life, your baby's feeding habits and food responses are greatly influenced by genes and environment. Some babies will eat anything in sight. Others, through some perversity of their own, develop strange food avoidances. In their concern, parents may unknowingly make the situation worse. Menus and tips in the previous chapters are designed to help avoid such problems before they start.

But what if your baby frustrates your every attempt to build good food habits? What if your child eats so little that you're convinced malnutrition is the next step? What if your little person greets each new food with stubborn resistance?

Your baby will never be just like your neighbor's baby who stuffs food down with gusto. You would not expect your child to walk or talk at the exact age the neighbor's child does, nor should you expect your child to have the same eating habits as your neighbor's child.

Let's look at ways of dealing with food and feeding which help to minimize the problem. Your child must have physical comforts attended to: dry diapers, warmth (but not too much warmth), comfortable, unrestricting, nonirritating clothes.

Learn all you can about your new baby. Don't worry about spoiling. A baby is never spoiled by too much of the right sort of attention. A baby needs to develop trust and to feel loved.

Talk to your baby fondly, pleasantly. Look into the tiny face. Seek the baby's eyes. Research has shown that babies hear high pitched voices more easily. Perhaps as a result of some primordial unconscious instinct, adults naturally tend to raise the pitch of their voices when they talk to an infant.

It is more difficult for the parents to establish a bond with some children, especially the baby who has been through a traumatic birth experience or who begins with a very low birth weight. The baby who has been through experiences like that may withdraw from human contact; the distressed infant keeps his eyes tightly closed and resists snuggling.

Feeding time can create real problems with a baby like this. Mother becomes tense, baby is tenser. The breasts may not let down well, or the baby may not nurse well. If the baby is bottle-fed, the frustrated parents may try to get more food into the baby by enlarging the hole in the nipple, causing the baby to choke or gag, and making the feeding problem even worse.

If you have these problems with your baby, fondling and cuddling are vital. Gentle light massage of each part of the baby's body will help him to relax. (Dr. Eva Reich calls this gentle massage "butterfly touch," starting with the forehead, neck, shoulders, arms, etc.) Hold your baby close to your body, the face turned toward you. Stroke gently from head to toe as you hold your child in this position. Baby will relax and so will you. Even the most robust, healthy, responsive child will benefit from this parental attention.

Feed the baby in an unhurried manner. Babyhood is a minute span in a person's life. But the growth and learning that take place are vast. Good or bad habits established in infancy can set the tone for life.

If your little one is unbending, refusing every tempting food you try, the best thing you can do is relax. That's tough advice to take. But the more fuss you create, the greater the problem may become.

You can find many ways to get around a child's eating problems. Perhaps the best way to begin, though, is to consider it just that: your baby's eating problem rather than your feeding problem. Whatever you do, resist the temptation to force-feed a child.

77

FOOD WITH LOVE

To avoid problems or to minimize a problem that has already begun, you should try to give your child as much love as possible. Provide an accepting and loving atmosphere at meals. If confusion, arguments, and upsets reign at mealtime, then anyone's appetite could be destroyed. While it is good to include your baby in the family meals, if there is much confusion and noise, it might be better to feed your child quietly alone before the rest of the family eats.

Remember, too, if you hold to a schedule as all supreme, you may automatically create an eating problem. Just as there is no hard-and-fast rule on starting foods, so mealtimes do not have to be confined to the usual schedules. Some toddlers don't want breakfast as soon as they get up in the morning. They may prefer to play around for an hour before they are ready to eat.

THE SLOW EATER

The slow eater who sits at the table from one meal to the next may actually be a victim of an overzealous parent who expects the child to eat too much. Provide extremely small servings and let the child ask for more. When your child starts dawdling or playing with the food, remove the plate and excuse the child from the table.

Toddlers' stomachs are small. Three large meals a day may overwhelm them. Divide their food into three small meals and two snacks. (Just be certain those snacks are a nutritious part of their food intake.)

Nothing will turn a baby against a new food quite so effectively as to have one of his elders turn up a nose and make a face at it. Caution the others in the family to leave what they don't like without fuss or fanfare. They are role models to the baby.

Give your child a small portion of each suitable food. If a protest comes forth, make no fuss. The food may land on the floor. Next time you serve the food, place an even smaller portion on the child's plate. Don't be surprised if you hear another protest, and the food is pushed off again. One day you may be astonished to find your child eating the offensive food as if it had always been his favorite.

Above all, don't force your child to eat something just because it is healthful. Substitute one food for another. Or disguise it in another form the baby may like.

You may be tempted at times to use sweets and desserts as rewards or to withhold them as punishment. This is unwise since it will surely make them become more desirable to your child. Provide only nutritious food, and even the most finicky child will eat only nutritious food.

If possible, withhold snacks for two hours prior to mealtime. Ask grandparents and friends not to bring candy, cookie, and cake treats. Ask them to bring fruit or dried fruit or some other nutritious favorite.

THE FINICKY EATER

Some children who previously have not been finicky may go through stages of preferring certain foods almost to the exclusion of all others. Yet generally, the child will receive adequate nourishment with the favorite food plus enough milk and vitamin supplements.

Sometimes the problem is the consistency of foods. The child will gag (almost deliberately) on lumpy cereal, thick puddings, stringy vegetables. Or the child will reject any food that does not meet a precise standard of crispness. Some children refuse milk—often not because they dislike the taste but because of some other factor. They object to the temperature or perhaps the texture.

If milk is a problem, serve it ice cold with an ice cube or try warmed milk. You can also switch the type of milk, from 2 percent to whole or back. Milk can be flavored with molasses, vanilla, or fruit. Finally, give the child milk in other forms: puddings, custards, cheeses, cream soups.

Sometimes a finicky child will insist that all foods be mixed together, or the child may want each food to be entirely separate. He may not even want one food on the same plate with another. To the child, these desires are not unreasonable. If you go along with them as games, you will both probably be happier.

Your physically and mentally healthy baby will eat enough, if provided, to stay alive. All babies are not (nor should they be) roly-poly butterballs. Roughly, a normal average 7½-pound (3.4-kilogram) baby should double birth weight by four or five months (to 15 pounds or 6.8 kilograms) and triple it by one year (to 22½ pounds or 10.2 kilograms). By 27 months, the birth weight is added again, and by four years old, the "average" child will weigh only five times the birth weight or 37½ pounds (17.0 kilograms).

You can see that in the three-year period from one to four years of age, the child will gain only about as much weight as was gained in the first year. Looking at it this way, you can readily see why appetite must taper off after a child celebrates the first birthday.

The young baby requires about 50 calories per pound of body weight. There are approximately 20 calories in every ounce of whole milk (cow's or human). The average one-year-old baby weighing 22½ pounds (10.2 kilograms) needs around 1,125 calories per day plus a slight edge for growth.

Let's say that the finicky baby's self-restricted diet is something like this:

BREAKFAST
½ cup orange juice	56 calories
1 small serving cooked cereal with 1 teaspoon honey	78 calories
1 glass milk	160 calories

LUNCH
1 hard-cooked egg	82 calories
1 slice whole wheat toast	89 calories
1 teaspoon butter	30 calories
1 tablespoon peanut butter	104 calories
1 glass milk	160 calories

DINNER
1½ ounces cooked ground beef	130 calories
1 glass milk	160 calories
	1,049 calories

An additional ½ cup of milk, a piece of fruit, cooked eggnog, a dish of pudding, and another slice of whole-grain toast will provide the caloric needs for this child. Furthermore, although limited and not ideal, this diet—along with vitamin supplements—is relatively well balanced. A little ingenuity on your part can make it even more varied or provide additional nutrients you feel are important.

Enrich the foods the child does like. Add wheat germ to the cereal. Spike the milk shakes with nourishing extra ingredients. Hide vegetables in a gelatin salad. Disguise a carrot, some squash, or even a sweet potato by adding it to a cooked eggnog.

The ingenious mother can put good nutrition over on an unsuspecting finicky child.

SIGNS OF POOR NUTRITION

Parents should learn to recognize the signs of poor nutrition (or of a half-hidden chronic illness which may be made worse by poor nutrition). Malnutrition has a snowball effect. For example, babies who live only on cow's milk in the second half of the first year and beyond often develop iron deficiency. If not recognized, iron deficiency causes crankiness, poor appetite, and pallor, and it could lead to more serious malnutrition, to susceptibility to illness, and to a general failure to thrive.

The signs of a worrisome poor nutrition are these:

- Chronic overweight or underweight
- Lethargy
- Crankiness
- Hair lacking in luster
- Poor skin tone
- Sleep disturbances (difficulty sleeping or too much sleeping)
- Frequent colds

Compare these signs to those of a healthy child: bright eyes, alert manner, clear complexion, lustrous hair, good skin elasticity, a generally good disposition, vigor, and energy.

THE ILL CHILD

Even a child who usually eats normally is likely to develop an eating problem during an illness. If your child's eating habits change radically and suddenly, get in touch with your medical advisor. The change could be just a normal stage of development or a natural short-term crankiness, or it could be a first sign of illness.

81

You can use some of the same methods for tempting the appetite of a sick child as you would use with the finicky child. Your doctor will be your guide as to what foods you should (or should not) feed a sick child.

The trick, overall, is to relax—even in situations that do not encourage relaxation. Sometimes the concerned parent has to pretend not to be concerned until the child changes an eating pattern all on his own.

CHAPTER TEN

THE RIGHT WEIGHT AT EVERY AGE

How fat is too fat? In infancy there is a fine line between malnutrition and good nutrition. The underfed baby is at risk since the brain cells are still multiplying and the insulating covering (the myelin sheath) surrounding the nerve fibers is being formed.

And fat cells do have some value. They act as insulators, protecting the infant from temperature changes and helping in the regulation of body temperature. They are energy reserves that can be called on in times of illness and stress. And they protect body organs from harm.

A baby who is normally active, thriving, healthy with a good appetite should not cause concern, especially if you are breastfeeding. Yet it is easy to become unduly concerned if the baby is chubby or skinny. Especially if the baby is chubby, you may be urged on all sides to cut down on feedings. That is no easy task—and it may not be advisable.

BREASTFEEDING AND WEIGHT GAIN

If breastfeeding is well established, you might be able to nurse at only one breast per feeding. Your baby may be satisfied, especially if you allow a full 15 to 20 minutes of nursing time.

Breast milk is unique. The early milk is thin and watery, while the later milk is rich and creamy. Barbara Hall reports in *Lancet* ("Changing Composition of Human Milk and Early Development of Appetite Control," April 5, 1975, p. 779) that the milk at the end of feeding contains four to five times as much fat and 1.5 times as much protein as the beginning milk. In the first five minutes of feeding, the baby takes in 60 percent of the milk volume but only 40 percent of the fat. In the next six minutes 26 percent of the volume is taken in and over 33 percent of the fat. Between the eleventh and sixteenth minutes of feeding, only 13 percent of the total volume is supplied, but nearly 25 percent of the fat.

On the basis of her research, Ms. Hall believes that the breastfed baby may control its feeding in response to the composition change in human milk. The change is a cue for the baby to stop feeding. She bases this idea on the fact that the baby will slow feeding as the richer milk comes in and gradually lose interest but if put to the other breast with its supply of thinner milk, will begin to nurse again with relish. The bottle-fed baby receives no such cue since the composition of formula is homogenous.

THE TRENDS IN INFANT WEIGHT GAIN

Pediatricians have been concerned with the trend toward earlier and earlier doubling of the birth weight in infancy. A 1976 study by C. G. Neumann ("Birthweight Doubling Times: A Fresh Look," *Pediatrics*, vol. 57, p. 469) showed that the mean time for doubling birth weight for bottle-fed babies is now 3.8 months. However, a study of fat thickness in babies done by Ann G. Ferris and others (*Pediatrics*, vol. 65, 1979) showed that though bottle-fed babies supplemented with solid food gained the most fat in the first three months, by six months their fat thickness had tapered off, and all babies, supplemented and unsupplemented, bottle-fed or breastfed, had about the same thickness of fat. The authors did find, though, that the fat of the breastfed babies was more solid and it was difficult to determine the thickness.

WHEN TO WORRY

The various studies are inconclusive. There is still disagreement as to when the proliferation of fat cells predisposes a child to lifelong obesity, whether in infancy or at adolescence. Therefore, no parent would want to jeopardize a baby's health and intellectual development to promote excessive leanness.

A study reported in *The Journal of Pediatrics* (D. Evans *et al*,

"Intellectual Development and Nutrition," 97:3, September 1980, pp. 358–363) compared intelligence scores of children who had been chronically malnourished with those of their siblings who were given supplemental feedings. The group which was supplemented had significantly higher intelligence test scores, by an average of at least 10 points.

But again, how fat is too fat? Too-fat babies are susceptible to upper respiratory infections—colds, bronchitis, pneumonia. They may be placid, inactive, and slower in motor development.

A study in Canada at the Human Nutrition Center, University of Sherbrooke, questions popular beliefs that overfeeding is the cause of obesity in infants.

INFANT INACTIVITY

In the Canadian study, the researchers found that the caloric intake per kilogram of body weight was actually lower for the heavy babies than for the lower-weight babies. These findings tend to affirm that obese babies are less active (or metabolize more slowly) than normal-weight babies. The researchers recommend caution in overreacting when a baby is fat by cutting food intake drastically.

At times, though, overfeeding, coupled with inactivity, may result in a fat baby.

A CASE STUDY

Baby Keith was one such baby. At five months of age, he was at the seventy-fifth percentile on growth charts in length. But he was well above the ninety-fifth percentile in weight for his age. He appeared to be a relatively quiet, inactive baby. According to his mother, he napped in the morning and slept from his noon meal until suppertime. He awakened once at night for feeding, usually sometime in the early morning.

He was eating about 4 to 5 tablespoons of dry cereal with fruit added, along with 3 to 4 ounces of milk in the morning. And he was also taking 4 ounces of sweetened juice for babies.

In midmorning, he occasionally had a teething biscuit. Then at noon, he would eat a whole jar of baby dinner. Along with the full jar of baby dinner, he had a 4- to 5-ounce bottle. Then he napped until suppertime. For supper he was eating approximately a cupful of potato and vegetable, both of which were salted and buttered. He also received one or two meat sticks and, in addition, he had a jar of fruit and another 4- to 5-ounce bottle of milk. At bedtime he received a full 8-ounce bottle.

His total milk intake in 24 hours equaled approximately 30 ounces. He had just been put on skim milk in an attempt to cut the number of calories.

According to Dr. Thomas A. Anderson, Professor of Pediatrics at the University of Iowa College of Medicine, diets intended to reduce the percent of body fat of infants four to eight months of age should provide 90 to 100 calories per kilogram (2.2 pounds) of body weight per day. This amount allows the infant to grow slowly out of obesity, without jeopardizing health.

Keith weighed approximately 20 pounds. Consequently, his caloric intake should have been somewhere between 900 and 1,000 calories per day. The 30 ounces of skim milk provided him with only 450 calories. This intake of solid foods was particularly high for a baby his age and provided him with somewhere in the vicinity of 300 to 400 or more calories per day. Yet all this did not add up to the 900 calories he should be taking in, nor did it provide sufficient intake of essential fatty acids. The only fat Keith was receiving was what he got from the meat sticks and the butter which was put on his vegetables, with no milk fats.

If Keith had received one can of formula (28 ounces or 840 ml.) diluted to make a total of 30 ounces (900 ml.), he would then be getting approximately 780 kilocalories from formula, which should be forming the bulk of his food intake at five months of age.

His mother needed to cut down the amount of cereal she fed him and use unsweetened juice. She was advised to eliminate the butter and salt used on the vegetables, to cut down on the potato, eliminate the meat sticks but use small amounts of blenderized puréed plain meat. She was told to use only unsweetened fruit, to eliminate the vegetable-and-beef dinner at noon, giving him only plain puréed vegetables.

These recommendations cut the caloric intake of the solid food he ate to about 200 calories. With this type of feeding regimen, he was expected slowly to outgrow the fatness he had developed.

He was not on a diet to lose weight. He was on a diet to outgrow the problem. As he grew, his mother was advised to increase his intake of solid foods slowly while maintaining his formula at the same level.

THE RISKS

Infancy is a risky period to play around with diets. The growth of the complex nervous system is too important. Of course, stuffing a child with large amounts of food and milk is not going to develop a super brain. But neither should a baby be starved to the point of damaging the nervous system or interfering with brain development—or even putting the development on a borderline. No one wants to jeopardize a baby's health because it's fashionable to be thin.

CHAPTER ELEVEN

ALL ABOUT ALLERGIES

If you or your husband or either of your families tend toward allergies, you will want to be especially careful to guard against allergy in your baby. Allergic reactions come in many forms and in response to a variety of substances. Food may be one cause of allergy, the one we are most concerned with here, although we must not overlook the fact that other types of allergies can interfere with good nutrition. For instance, hay fever which causes a stuffed-up nose may prevent a baby from nursing well.

Each person develops individual allergies, so just because you are allergic to a particular substance does not necessarily mean your baby will be allergic to it. If the baby becomes allergic, it may be to something that does not affect you at all.

MILK AND ALLERGIES

If you feel your baby is liable to develop an allergy, it would be an especially good idea to breastfeed. It is unlikely that your baby will develop an allergy to your milk (though, rarely, some substance you eat may cause trouble).

Eczema used to be the most common form of allergy in young babies. Fat babies seemed to be the most prone to develop eczema. Then researchers discovered that eczema correlated with the use of fat-free milk.

For some years, doctors were putting bottle-fed babies on skim milk to prevent their getting overly fat. Skim milk contains no fat so these babies were being deprived of essential fatty acids needed for myelinization of the nervous system and for healthy skin.

Once eczema or any other allergy starts it may be very difficult to control or to eliminate. There are a number of steps you can take which help in some degree to prevent your baby from developing allergies in the first place.

ALLERGENIC FOODS

Some foods are especially liable to be allergy producing. Proteins seem to be the most likely to produce allergy, especially the protein of milk, eggs, and cereal (usually wheat). The fruits which are most likely to cause allergy are strawberries and citrus fruits.

Beans and celery are among allergenic vegetables, while shellfish and pork are the fish and meat to suspect most readily. Some nuts or certain spices, such as cinnamon, may be troublesome, as well as honey produced from flowers whose pollens are a source of allergy.

AVOIDING ALLERGIES
FROM THE BEGINNING

Delay starting your baby on solid foods as long as you reasonably can. When you do start solids, use first the ones which are least likely to produce allergy. When you introduce the baby to an important new food like egg, which is known to be highly allergenic, give it very gradually. Start with the egg yolk only, just ¼ (1 ml.) to ½ teaspoon (2 ml.) the first day, 1 teaspoon (5 ml.) the second day, 2 teaspoons (10 ml.) the third day, and so on, until the baby is taking a whole yolk. Even then, you will want to restrict him to no more than one yolk a day until he is one year old, and then begin whole eggs gradually.

You may use this gradual introduction to all of the most allergy-producing foods, such as orange juice, wheat, etc. Also be sure that any new food is given to the baby at least twice in any one week. Repeating the food regularly gives you an opportunity to observe any allergic reaction. And it prevents the risk of encountering a later, more severe allergic reaction.

Sometimes a food will produce allergy in one form but not in another. For example, the baby may tolerate cooked milk or cheese but not fresh milk.

Another point to remember is that if one food of a family of foods causes allergy, another food from the same family is liable to cause trouble also. For example, a baby who is allergic to oranges is liable to be allergic to other citrus fruits; if to broccoli, then to other members of the cabbage family.

If you are breastfeeding and you eat foods to which your baby is allergic, the baby might have a reaction. Usually, foods that agree with the mother when she eats them (in moderation) should cause her baby no trouble. But if your baby has allergies, such as to eggs or wheat, see if your doctor thinks you should eliminate that particular food from your diet while you are nursing.

If your baby receives an excess of B vitamins in infancy, his susceptibility to allergy may be increased. Since the young baby receives B vitamins from milk, cereals, meats, egg yolks, and other components of the diet, it is a good idea to give a vitamin supplement containing only A, C, and D (if needed). Don't give a multivitamin preparation unless it is specifically ordered by the doctor. In general, vitamin drops should not be given in addition to the vitamins a baby gets from the milk of a mother who has a good vitamin intake or from a complete formula. In a particular instance, of course, the physician may advise otherwise.

Your baby may develop any one of a number of forms of allergy. The typical symptoms include hives, itching, diarrhea, and other gastrointestinal disturbances, or asthma. In any case, the development of allergy requires the services of a physician. If you have started your baby's diet as recommended, adding only one new food at a time, it will be far easier for the doctor to pinpoint the cause of the allergy and to recommend a course of therapy.

BECOMING FOOD CONSCIOUS

Furthermore, if your child has food allergies, you will need to become food conscious. You must be aware of the contents of any commercial foods you give your child to be sure they do not contain some substance which will cause allergic reaction. For example, the baby who is allergic to corn may react to corn oil or corn syrup. Wheat is particularly difficult to avoid because most breads, gravies, meat loaf mixes, soups, puddings, sauces, and even some processed meats contain wheat. Most of the combination-dinner baby foods contain wheat in some form.

You cannot always rely on the label. In some instances, the manufacturer is not required to specify all of the contents, particularly if the food is one made from a standard recipe. In other cases, the label may state only "cereal added," without indicating what sort of cereal. You might as well plan to do a great deal of your own cooking from the original ingredients. Get into the habit of reading all labels, too, to be sure there are no additives which might create one more problem.

HIDDEN ALLERGIES

But what if you are already faced with a chronically unwell child? Many families of young children have been faced with the frustrating problem of chronic unwellness—and this in spite of faultless care.

A baby may be sick with a runny nose, ear infection, sore throat, all types of respiratory infections, one after another.

In fact, allergy can strike any system of the body, the urinary system (older children who are bedwetters are sometimes suffering from allergy) or the nervous system (hyperactive children may be allergic).

In a national survey it was found that one third of chronic childhood conditions were due to allergies.

After the pediatrician has ruled out underlying medical problems, deprivation and malnutrition, iron or vitamin deficiency, there remains another plausible cause for a chronic illness: allergy.

Skin testing is not especially useful in identifying food allergies. But because food allergies are the most common allergies in children under the age of three, careful evaluation is needed.

A CASE STUDY

In one such frustrating situation, the young mother of two boys, ages 18 months and 7 years, was faced with children who were both chronically unwell. Winters were a nightmare of colds, ear infections, and bronchitis. Summers were not much better, as the children broke out in rashes and suffered from diarrhea. The younger boy struggled with diaper rash. Both slept poorly at night and were overly active during the day. The older boy wet the bed.

This mother, naturally, was discouraged. She had tried to do everything right, nursing them both, preparing baby food from the best products available at the local food co-op, giving them loving supervision. Her family physician was nutritionally oriented and conservative in using drugs. But he was stymied.

Because her husband's family had a history of allergies, the mother became convinced that her children were victims of allergies. With the backing of her physician, she sought the assistance of a nurse-practitioner to help her find the answer. Most physicians do not have the time to carry out the kind of in-depth study and close support needed in dealing with obscure allergies. A consulting nurse or dietician working with the family may make the difference between success and failure.

The children were observed from head to toe for size, color, skin problems, level of activity, eyes (dark circles, puffiness, redness, alertness, etc.), unusual gestures or habits (pulling at ears, rubbing nose, rubbing eyes, throat clearing, etc.).

The home environment was assessed: the location, type of house, kind of heating, furnishings, plants, and animals. Gas heaters, dust-blowing hot air heat, dust-collecting overstuffed furniture, thick carpets, pets, dampness leading to the growth of molds and mildews, all can cause allergy or be a factor in the control of allergy.

The first steps in dealing with allergy-caused illness are these:

- Cover mattresses.
- Eliminate feather pillows.
- Isolate pets.
- Provide air filters for heating systems.
- Get rid of dust-collecting furniture and carpets or clean them daily.
- Cut down pollen-causing plants.

The next action in this case was for the parents to maintain a journal on each child. Every day, the parents took notes on the weather, the temperature, the wind. They kept an hour-by-hour account of the food the children ate, the places they visited, their activity, behavior, and status of health.

At the end of two weeks, the nurse-practitioner evaluated the journals to see if patterns emerged.

Through the scrutiny of the advisors, an obvious cause might become immediately apparent. But if no such clear-cut cause is seen, then the parents must institute an elimination diet. This is a slow and tedious process requiring dedication on the part of the parents and close supervision from the nurse, dietician, and doctor.

This young mother was committed to ferreting out the cause of her children's ill health. So she started them on a basic hypoallergenic diet in order to simplify the process. The diet was extremely limited and required considerable ingenuity on her part.

She had to read every label. She had to prepare most foods herself. She could not even rely on many of the vitamin preparations. The boys' physician had prescribed vitamins A, C, and D as a precaution against the diet's limitations. Yet the complete contents of the vitamin preparation are seldom listed on the package—and some of them could contribute to the allergic reactions. Thus the boys' mother used Ascorbic Acid Powder, U.S.P., and cod liver oil, all of which contain no unknown ingredients.

At the end of the two weeks, both boys were free of infection, and their behavior had improved. The older boy had even stopped wetting the bed.

Gradually, their mother added new foods to the basic hypoallergenic diet. The process was a little like starting a baby on solids for the first time.

At first she added only one new food a week. If there were no problems, she continued the food. If a child developed trouble after she added a new food, she withdrew it and tried it again at a later date.

At first, the mother needed twice-weekly guidance in making decisions on foods to add and on the development of possible problems. Gradually, however, she became more and more capable of making the additions on her own with only occasional contact with the nurse and her usual contact with the doctor.

During vacations, the children were not given any new foods, since traveling and new surroundings were enough of a change without running the risk of adding an allergy-producing food.

This diet started in August. That first winter was their healthiest since birth. By the third winter, these two children seemed to be the only ones in the neighborhood who were not sick.

Their major allergies turned out to be to sugar, grapes and grape

products (both had loved grape juice), and various refined manufactured foods. The latter allergies were presumed to be to some
substances contained in the foods such as colorings, flavorings, or
preservatives.

The second summer, the younger child wanted only juices to
drink. Yet his favorite drinks gave him occasional diarrhea and a
red bottom. The nurse recommended diluting the juices with water
in which small amounts of barley or oatmeal had been dissolved or
cooked. Barley and oatmeal waters are soothing, and the child was
able to continue drinking the juices he craved during that hot
summer.

When a third child was born, the mother totally breastfed and
delayed solids until late in the first year. She was alert to signs of
allergy and was able to avoid the problems that had beset the other
children.

At last her care and concern for her children had produced
results. Relatives could no longer say "If breastfeeding and natural
foods are so good, how come your children are always sick?"

HYPERACTIVITY

Allergy to ordinary refined sugar (sucrose) may be far more
widespread than has been recognized. Dr. William Crook, a pediatric allergist, says sugar is the first thing he eliminates. Foods high in
sugar do seem to set off a cycle of hyperactivity in susceptible
individuals. Certainly, the increase in the number of hyperactive
children parallels the increased sugar consumption in this country,
as well as the increased use of artificial flavors and colorings.

Dr. Benjamin Feingold claimed success with his salicylate-free
diet for hyperactive children. Salicylates are found naturally in
many foods, and he believes they can cause hyperactivity as a
symptom of allergic reaction.

Other researchers have questioned Dr. Feingold's conclusions.
But many parents of hyperactive children are convinced that his
diet works. Why the discrepancies? Perhaps in some cases the
cause of hyperactivity is salicylate-containing foods, food flavorings, and colorings. In other cases, the cause may be sugar or some
other allergen, perhaps even environmental factors.

ALLERGY COOKING

Because allergies to milk, wheat, and eggs are the most difficult to cope with, and because nearly every prepared food contains one of these, our recipes have been designed to meet problems caused by these particular allergies. Special notations have been made at the beginning of many recipes to indicate that they do *not* contain ingredients (eggs, wheat, milk) that tend to cause allergic reactions.

MILK ALLERGY

In most recipes, you can substitute water for milk, although the texture of the food will be changed. Milk substitutes such as soy milk may work fine. Milk is particularly difficult to avoid since nonfat dry milk, whey butter, and cream are added to many foods including processed meats and margarines.

EGG ALLERGY

In general, you will probably have to avoid recipes that use eggs. Cornstarch or tapioca may be used to thicken puddings. There is a product called "Chone" which is an imitation of whole egg powder, made of safflower oil, rice flour, and nonfat milk solids. It is said to be usable in recipes that require eggs, but check with your medical advisor regarding its use. It is available in pharmacies or write General Mills Chemical, Inc., Dept. FH, 4620 West 77 Street, Minneapolis, MN 55435.

WHEAT ALLERGY

Most breads contain some wheat, even though they may be labeled "oatmeal," "corn," or even "rye bread." Unless otherwise noted on the package, rye wafers, such as hardtack, contain only rye, salt, and water. The heavy pumpernickel or rye loaves are often made only of rye, water, yeast, and salt. Check the label, or if in doubt, check with the bakery.

In place of wheat bread crumbs called for in many recipes, use crumbled rye wafers, pure rye bread crumbs, crushed corn flakes, crushed potato chips, dehydrated potato flakes, or cornmeal.

To thicken gravies and puddings without wheat, use potato starch, cornstarch, or dehydrated potato flakes.

WHEAT FLOUR SUBSTITUTES

The end results of a product containing one of these substitutes will differ from the original in texture.

For each cup of flour, use one of the following:

½ cup (125 ml.) barley flour
½ cup (125 ml.) cornstarch and ½ cup (125 ml.) rye flour
½ cup (125 ml.) cornstarch and ½ cup (125 ml.) potato flour
½ cup (125 ml.) cornstarch and ½ cup (125 ml.) rice flour
½ cup (125 ml.) rye flour and ½ cup (125 ml.) potato flour
1 cup (250 ml.) soy flour and ¾ cup (180 ml.) potato flour (Use full 1¾-cup amount here in place of 1 cup usual flour.)
⅔ cup (160 ml.) rye flour and ⅓ cup (80 ml.) potato flour

Allergy is a pervasive problem. Combatting allergy takes dedication and astute observation, but the rewards will be great and obvious.

CHAPTER TWELVE
FOOD FOR VEGETARIAN BABIES

A vegetarian diet can be managed, and managed beautifully, for a baby, but it does require some serious knowledge of nutrition. It ought not to be a casual endeavor.

You have to work at vegetarianism for small children. Their growth is rapid, and their appetites sometimes quite small. It can be difficult to feed a vegetarian child the concentrated nutrients and the calories essential to the right growth. Probably a serious vegetarian family ought to work in cooperation with a dietician who can overlook individual problems and who can see exactly how each child is doing nutritionally.

THE ADVANTAGES

Vegetarianism can give a child definite long-range advantages.

In bringing up your children as vegetarians, you may be preparing them for the necessary future. Vegetarians are eating lower on the food chain. They are making an efficient use of available protein. Animal protein, especially as it is produced in the United States, will never be an efficient source of food. A beef animal, for instance, must consume great amounts of food itself in relation to the amount of food it will eventually produce. The farm land required to feed one family is considerably less if that family is vegetarian.

In places where food is scarce, people have tended to be vegetarians out of necessity. They cannot afford meat, and their beleaguered farm land must be used to produce directly for people, not indirectly to produce food for animals who will become food for people only at some later time. Meat is a rare luxury in most parts of the world.

Probably as the world becomes more crowded everywhere, and the environment becomes more fragile, greater numbers of people will give up eating meat—or certainly give up eating meat in large, daily quantities. They may well find meat prohibitively expensive, and the philosophical arguments will undoubtedly carry ever greater weight as their truth becomes more evident.

Many people become vegetarians, for instance, when they see what cruelties are inflicted upon animals in the name of making meat a more efficient—and more profitable—food. Eating meat can be disgusting if one thinks of the unnatural life and death of the animal. Some think of meat-eating as an irreligious act.

Others become vegetarians out of self-interest. Meat is liable to be contaminated with pesticide residue, more so than other foods. Sick animals may be dosed up on antibiotics and other drugs before they are slaughtered.

Vegetarians can hope to keep healthy, strong cardiovascular systems; they also run less risk than others of gout or of cancer of the colon.

Vegetarians are less liable to get fat. They are almost never obese, and knowledgeable vegetarians find their diets to be satisfying, tasty, and full of variety.

THE RESTRICTIONS

Some forms of vegetarianism, however, are not appropriate for small children.

The raw foodists, fruitarians, and some other radical vegetarians live on extremely restricted diets. Some refuse to kill living plants any more than they would kill living animals for their food, so they live on fallen fruits. They may live almost directly from nature, without cooking or preparing foods. Or they may live almost exclusively on one or two central foods.

It isn't easy for them. The restrictions they impose can be so great that these vegetarians may knowingly sacrifice health in exchange for a philosophical benefit. That sort of sacrifice cannot rightly be imposed on a small child. Besides the fact that a person should be capable of an independent decision before embarking on a physical sacrifice of that magnitude, an extremely restricted vegetarian diet is also going to harm a child much more than it would harm a full-grown adult.

The child's rapid growth requires adequate protein and sufficient overall calories. An adult eats to have energy and to maintain a static state of health. A child eats for those reasons, too, but the child must also keep growing and developing in complex patterns.

The vegetarian child runs a risk of taking on so few calories that the available protein is all used up in energy, leaving no ''extra'' protein to support the child's growth.

Primarily, the development of the nervous system is incomplete until the child is at least fifteen to eighteen months of age. Inadequate protein prior to that time can compromise development and cause the child difficulty forever after.

Vegans are complete vegetarians. They eat no animal products at all, no meat and also no milk, eggs, or even honey. But they do not necessarily live on an extremely restricted or self-damaging diet. They can eat a wide variety of foods, and their goal may well be personal health without any other motive they would see as sacrifice.

A child can be reared in a vegan family as long as the child's parents are knowledgeable and conscientious. There is no room for junk food in a vegan diet, and there is little opportunity for random food selection. Food requires forethought for everyone, the more so for vegans.

Many other vegetarians, probably most, are far more liberal than vegans. Lacto-ova-vegetarians allow, as the name implies, milk and eggs. They may even eat seafood and poultry occasionally, and they are not liable to suffer from debilitating dietary restrictions.

Some problems may remain for vegetarian parents rearing their children as vegetarians, even if the parents do not plan on any unduly restrictive diet. One problem is that vegetarians ought to be eating a great variety and large amounts of legumes, vegetables, and whole grains. Adults usually enjoy the variety and the filling and satisfying nature of their vegetarian diets. But they know they must eat these foods in particular patterns in order to take in enough complete usable protein.

The problem arises with a child who has a small stomach and

often a smaller appetite. The child may not be physically able to eat the food combinations necessary to optimal health. A picky eater is a double problem for concerned parents who want to remain vegetarians.

CONSTRUCTING A
VEGETARIAN DIET

The basis of the problem is this. All living things as we know them—and that includes our own human bodies—are built out of complex protein. Protein, in turn, is complex because it is constructed out of 22 amino acids. When the body needs its protein building blocks, it can generate its own amino acids, 14 times out of 22. The other 8 amino acids (9 for a baby) cannot be made "in house." They must be constructed from the amino acids in the food that a person eats.

Meat contains all the amino acids that a person needs, since meat comes from another animal of similar basic protein structure. That's the one great advantage of eating other animals. A person who eats meat is getting "complete" protein, or in other words a complete setup of all the amino acids that human beings cannot make within their own bodies.

Plants can also provide protein, but not with all the amino acids in the right pattern and in the right amount. Human chemistry does not coordinate as precisely with plant chemistry as it does with the chemistry of other animals.

Plant protein is called "incomplete." It can become complete in combination with other plant foods that mix and match amino acids so that they come out right for the human body.

The right combinations are nearly mathematical. Think of food as existing in five groups:

1. Milk and dairy products
2. Grains (flours, cereals, rice, corn, pasta)
3. Legumes (beans, peas, and lentils)
4. Seeds and nuts
5. Vegetables (especially the dark green leafy vegetables)

To make up a complete usable protein, one would need to select food from these groups in patterns:

- Group 1 with group 2
- Group 2 with group 3
- Group 3 with group 4
- Group 4 with group 5

Cereal with milk correctly combines groups 1 and 2. A peanut butter sandwich combines groups 2 and 4. Add pea soup with the sandwich, and group 3 comes in.

SUBSTITUTES FOR ANIMAL PRODUCTS

Some vegetarian main dishes are almost direct substitutes for meat, so that the food groups are combined for a complete protein all in one main dish. Eggplant lasagne, for instance, combines the food groups, and its taste is almost indistinguishable from the ordinary ground-beef lasagne.

The concept of the exact meat substitute is really unnecessary to the true vegetarian, who has no desire to think of food in terms of artificial meats or meat substitutes. The commercial meat substitutes may help to begin a new changeover to vegetarian eating. They replicate the type of meals that the former meat-eater is used to. But these meat substitutes are essentially convenience foods, and not needed in the long run.

Instead, the vegetarian can think in terms of the best possible sources for the nutritional needs of the human body, especially for children.

The American Dietetic Association has isolated particular nutritional deficiencies that have plagued vegetarian families whose children's diets were not planned well enough. The reports even uncovered cases of kwashiorkor among vegan infants in the United States (the reports covering Chicago and Cleveland only). Kwashiorkor is a severe nutritional disorder almost unheard of in the Western world. Poorly nourished vegan children were often found to be suffering from rickets. Or they were short and light for their ages, and some lacked the energy and intelligence they ought to have had.

These dietary deficiences do not have to happen. For small children, the particular nutritional needs that the American Dietetic Association uncovered most often are as follows:

101

- Calcium
- Riboflavin
- Vitamin B$_{12}$
- Vitamin D
- Iron

CALCIUM

To avoid these problems, the vegetarian mother would be particularly wise to breastfeed her baby. That's the natural and right way to feed an infant from the beginning. Otherwise, a vegan mother who wished to stay away from all animal products would be forced to use soy-based formula. Soy formula can keep a baby alive and well, but it is not as good as formula based on cow's milk, and certainly not anywhere near as good for a human baby as human mother's milk.

The other common milk substitute for vegans is based on sesame seed.

Check to make sure that any commercial formula of this sort that you use is fortified with vitamins A, B$_{12}$, D, and K and also fortified with calcium. A commercial soy-based formula will also have been treated in ways that guarantee the quality of the protein. For these reasons, we recommend commercial formula only when the baby cannot be breastfed—and not any of the homemade soy or sesame seed formula recipes.

Human milk is superior to all of them, and when a mother succeeds in breastfeeding her baby, she does not need to worry about the calcium, vitamins, and minerals in the baby's milk. The mother needs to keep her own food intake high—in both calories and protein—to be certain her milk supply remains high. But as long as the nursing mother herself is eating a respectably nutritious diet, the necessary nutrients will be there for her baby.

After weaning, we strongly recommend that the vegetarian child continue to drink milk either in the form of cow's milk or, if that animal product is not acceptable, in the form of well-fortified soy milk. Fortified soy milk is by far the best non-animal source of calcium, but there are others.

Other non-milk foods can help to provide calcium in a vegetarian diet, and they would be right for pregnant women and for nursing mothers, as well as for introduction to small children:

- Almonds
- Blackstrap molasses
- Broccoli
- Carob flour
- Collard greens
- Dandelion greens
- Kale
- Legumes
- Mustard and turnip greens
- Rutabagas
- Sesame seed meal and spread
- Soy flour and other forms of soybeans
- Tofu (based on soybean curd)

RIBOFLAVIN

Many of these same foods help to meet the need for riboflavin. Three common vegetarian food groups ought to contain sufficient riboflavin: the dark green leafy vegetables, legumes, and whole grains. Nutritional (or brewer's) yeast is also good in reasonable amounts, and it can also supply a good source of vitamin B_{12}.

VITAMINS

Mostly, vitamins B_{12} and D must come into a vegetarian diet through supplements as these vitamins are not available in ordinary vegetarian foods. The American Dietetic Association does not recommend using seaweed or fermented soy for vitamin B_{12} supplements since these products are not reliable. Soybean milk and some of the commercial meat substitutes, however, are adequately fortified with both vitamin B_{12} and vitamin D, and for lacto-ova-vegetarians, these vitamins are available in milk products and in eggs.

Vitamin D is also manufactured from sunlight. The child who plays in the sun every day will get enough vitamin D.

IRON

The remaining nutrient problem for many vegetarian children is lack of iron. So many Americans suffer from dietary lack of iron that it is a national problem for both vegetarians and for meat-eaters.

It is important to find good food sources of iron for virtually every meal. Some of the iron sources we have listed before, and the non-meat sources bear repeating since they are crucial to a good vegetarian diet:

- Blackstrap molasses
- Beet greens
- Chard
- Dates
- Dried peaches and apricots
- Egg yolks
- Garbanzo beans (chick-peas)
- Kale
- Lentils
- Lima beans
- Millet
- Pinto beans and other legumes
- Prunes and prune juice
- Pumpkin seeds
- Rice
- Split peas
- Tofu and other soybean products
- Torula yeast
- Wheat germ

Equally important to iron-rich foods are foods that aid the human body's absorption of iron. Meat is one of these foods, but so is ascorbic acid or vitamin C foods, and vegetarians ought to include in every meal a fruit or vegetable that is high in vitamin C. These foods are valuable on their own, and like so many foods, their value is enhanced by the combinations in which one eats them.

The point is to be very careful in making up a vegetarian diet for a baby.

We recommend that, besides consulting a dietician, you keep a small library on the subject. Frances Moore Lappe's *Diet for a Small*

Planet is the classic book on vegetarianism. You will also want to consult *The Farm Vegetarian Cookbook*, or one of the other good books on vegetarian cuisine. One book concentrates on a non-meat diet for children. It is Sharon Yntema's *Vegetarian Baby*. Although it sometimes hammers the obvious (pointing out that one will need a knife with which to chop vegetables), it has at least the virtues of being thorough and specific.

Thorough knowledge, good planning, and excellent cooking are the hallmarks of a successful vegetarian upbringing.

As a vegetarian parent, you cannot ever afford to fill a child's small stomach and to satisfy a child's slight appetite with any foods of less than excellent nutritional value. A child might well enjoy foods that offer low nourishment and high calories. But these foods might push aside other necessary components of a vegetarian diet.

What the child really needs, most of the time, is small servings— but small servings of a wide variety of carefully selected foods.

The child can be a successful, healthy, brilliant vegetarian for a whole long lifetime—and can thank the parents who must work hard to pull it all off, even against the pressures of a meat-and-potatoes culture.

CHAPTER THIRTEEN

NOURISHMENT BEFORE YOUR BABY'S BIRTH

An unborn child needs good nourishment, too. The best time to begin a good nutritional program starts long before birth.

Think of the growth that occurs in those first nine months before your baby is ready to live in the outside world. There is no time when a person grows more rapidly.

In an astonishing way, an unborn baby is growing intellectually as well as physically. During the last three months before birth, about 75 percent of the brain cells are formed.

What can the mother do to help her unseen baby?

That rapid and marvelous growth imposes a special nutritional stress that we do know about.

There is a truth of life and of nutrition. The more crucial and more rapid the growth, the greater is the nutritional stress. The greater the stress, the greater and more urgent is the need for good nourishment.

Now the pregnant woman cannot provide her baby with nutrients that are not available to her. The unborn baby is not a part of the mother's body. Nor is the baby a parasite in the strict biological sense of the word. The baby's system cannot leech calcium from the mother's teeth, nor essential calories or proteins from her muscles.

In fact, during the last weeks of pregnancy, as the mother's body makes physical preparation for breastfeeding, it will store deep fat layers even if it must do so at the expense of cutting daily nourishment to the fetus. If a woman were starving, her unborn baby would starve. If she were lacking in nutrients, her baby would suffer.

The unborn baby, then, is entirely dependent on the day-to-day "extra" nourishment the mother can provide.

EARLY PREGNANCY

A woman hoping to become a mother should pay attention to her food selection from the beginning—even before her child is conceived.

In the first trimester, the first three months, of pregnancy, the fertilized ovum grows to be a miniature human being, lengthening to 8 centimeters (just over 3 inches) and weighing 28 grams (almost 1 ounce). The developing ovum and the early embryo maintain that rapid growth by digesting secretions from the endometrium, the soft spongy lining of the uterus. Thus, this very early embryonic development is dependent upon the mother's nutritional condition at conception. The mother's good nutrition, therefore, is important even before she decides to have a baby.

The first three months of pregnancy are characterized by a decrease in the mother's appetite. Often these first infamous months are accompanied by morning sickness. At this stage, the mother may tolerate carbohydrates when nothing else will stay down.

The key to comfort is for her to keep something in her uneasy stomach at all times; that will help to prevent recurring nausea. Just before rising in the morning, a woman may particularly need some help of that sort; it can be useful to have dry toast, crackers, or another dry carbohydrate on the bedside table.

The placenta, the unique organ which provides nourishment to the fetus, begins to function about the eighth week of pregnancy, and it is fully functioning by the twelfth week. Through the membranes of the placenta, the nutrients provided by the mother's blood pass into the fetal circulation to be used for growth and development. In the same manner, waste products from the baby are passed into the mother's bloodstream to be cleared through her liver and kidneys.

The placenta is actually an embryonic organ. It is formed from cells encircling the developing embryo. As these cells digest the endometrium, the embryo within its sack of membranes becomes attached to the wall of the uterus. The mother's veins and arteries open into the spaces formed by this process. The baby's placental veins and arteries hang in these spaces, where they can receive nourishment from the mother's blood.

There is no direct mingling of the maternal and fetal blood supplies. They are always separate and distinct. The essential exchange takes place through the membranes that form the baby's blood vessels.

THE "GOLDEN MONTHS" OF PREGNANCY

In the second trimester of pregnancy, the mother's appetite increases, and she feels better. These are the golden months of pregnancy. In the well-nourished woman, the placenta grows rapidly, acting as a clearinghouse for wastes and for nutrients. It is also a sort of storehouse for nutrients.

The placenta also manufactures hormones which cause changes within the mother's body. One very important change is a large increase in the mother's blood volume. That increase helps to ensure good nutrition for the fetus. Each beat of the mother's heart sends fountains of blood spurting into the spaces of the placenta. The mother's nutrient-bearing blood comes into forceful contact with the baby's placental blood vessels. Nourishment is virtually rushing and pushing to get through.

A good nourishing diet is vitally important to the placenta, so that it can grow and function as it ought to. The mother has to be well-enough nourished to maintain the greatly expanded blood volume that she needs to grow a healthy baby.

NEARING THE END OF PREGNANCY

During the third trimester of pregnancy, the baby's organs continue to develop. The infant liver begins to function, and it will be storing iron for use after birth. The baby's brain cells multiply rapidly at this point, and in the last few weeks, the baby's body adds subcutaneous tissue. The baby is growing a protective insulation against the first stressful weeks of life. If the mother eats poorly in these crucial months, her baby may develop fewer brain cells. The baby may be born at a lower weight than normal, and may be less well developed than nature meant.

The poorly nourished mother can become ill herself. If too little protein or sodium is available to keep the blood expanded, the blood volume drops. Fluid escapes into the mother's tissues, causing sudden swelling. The mother's body, in its attempt to maintain placental circulation, will respond by constricting the blood vessels. Given this state of affairs, the mother's blood pressure will rise suddenly—and dangerously.

This condition is called toxemia. It is a dangerous condition for both the mother and the baby. A large, healthy placenta pulls forth large amounts of hormones and functions well only with a well-expanded—and well-nourished—maternal blood volume.

But the mother has to continue eating a well-balanced diet containing ample protein, calories, and nutrients. And for the pregnant woman, salt is a necessary element. Studies by such experts as Doctors Leon Cherey and Margaret Robinson show that salt intake should not be restricted during pregnancy.

THE BASIC DIET

What should the pregnant woman eat?

She can start with a good basic diet, one which provides her with at least 300 more calories than she would normally consume. Consider the hypothetical "average" woman aged 19 to 22, 5 feet 4 inches (163 cm.) tall, weighing 120 pounds (55 kg.). The Recommended Dietary Allowance for her daily calories during pregnancy is 2,400 (as revised in 1980 by the Food and Nutrition Board of the National Academy of Science National Research Council). Although a daily protein intake of 74 grams is recommended, many experts (including Agnes Higgins, the Director of the Montreal Diet Dispensary, and Dr. Thomas H. Brewer, President of SPUN, the Society to Protect the Unborn Through Nutrition) consider this amount much too low and believe that 100 grams of daily protein is a safer figure.

The underweight or very active woman will need more protein and calories, as will the young teen-ager about to become a mother. The mother of twins will need even more in the way of extra protein and additional calories.

Pregnancy is not the time for any woman to try to reduce her weight by restrictive dieting. The average and perfectly normal weight gain during pregnancy might go up to 30 or even 40 pounds. This is not to say that an obese woman ought not to take the opportunity of pregnancy to change her ways. She may be able to manage for the sake of her baby to change from a lifetime of bad eating. If she can change over to a good nutritional pattern, she will help herself, too.

According to Dr. Brewer, the leading proponent of good prenatal nutrition, the obese woman who cuts excess fats from her diet but still consumes adequate protein, carbohydrates, and other nutrients may safely gain less than the average during pregnancy without harm to her baby or herself. The key is to eat right and to let the weight gain be as it should.

It is dangerous to restrict calories, especially in the last weeks of pregnancy. By restricting calories, a woman might also restrict good nourishment just at a time when she and her baby need that nourishment most.

But if a pregnant woman determines not to restrict calories, that is not a license for her to indulge in junk food. The pregnant woman does not need calories purely for their own sake. She needs the concentrated good nutrition and calories of a well-balanced diet.

Here is a basic daily menu for an adult pregnant woman:

- 4 cups milk (whole or skim)
- 2 or more servings meat, poultry, fish, or a vegetarian combination of legumes, vegetables, and whole grains
  (Include at least one serving of liver per week, or for the adult vegetarian woman, other iron-rich foods.)
- 2 eggs
- 1 or more servings dark green leafy vegetables (broccoli, brussels sprouts, dandelion greens, endive, beet greens, spinach)
- 1 or more servings deep yellow vegetables (carrots, squash, yams)
  Serve some raw vegetables every day.
- 1 or more servings of a fruit that is high in vitamin C (cantaloupe, grapefruit, oranges and orange juice, raspberries and strawberries)
- 1 or more servings of a vegetable or other fruit that is high in

vitamin C (potato, tomato and tomato juice, cabbage, broccoli, kale, collard greens, turnip greens, mustard greens,
brussels sprouts, cauliflower, fresh green or red sweet pepper)
- 4 to 5 servings of whole grain cereal, bread, rice, or enriched
pasta
- Fats in moderation (butter, margarine, oils, shortenings)

SPECIAL DIETS

For nursing mothers, pregnant teen-agers, and mothers expecting
twins, add to the basic diet:

- 1 additional cup milk
- 1 additional serving of meat, poultry, fish, cheese, or legumes

Pregnancy is time for a vegetarian mother to pay particularly
close attention to her diet. She will need extra calcium either in the
form of milk or from plenty of leafy green vegetables. And she
must be sure to eat combinations of legumes, vegetables, and
whole grains to allow herself the complete, body-usable protein she
will need to nourish herself and her baby.

The nursing mother should continue to follow the recommended
diet for pregnancy, adding another 200 calories per day, in the form
of an additional 8 ounces of milk or the equivalent.

The woman who eats in good patterns while she is pregnant and
lactating will find benefits to herself as well as to her baby. She will
be more ready for an easy labor and delivery. She is more likely to
recover rapidly, too, even if she does have a difficult delivery or a
cesarean section. She is less prone to infection, and, as a nursing
mother, she produces more milk.

The infant who is well nourished before birth will come into the
world larger, healthier, and more resistant to illnesses. Statistically,
the well-nourished baby is able to eat and sleep well and is
supposed to be of a better temper, easier to care for.

You cannot guarantee good health only by good eating, but you
can make your chances better. And if you are lucky enough to give
birth to a healthy baby, you can take some of the credit. Good
nourishment before birth can be the beginning of a lifetime of good
nourishment—and of a good lifetime.

CHAPTER FOURTEEN
ACTION AGAINST ENVIRONMENTAL HAZARDS

When DDT first came into use, it was hailed as the answer to the world's agricultural problems. Instead, it set off an ecological nightmare. The balance of nature was disturbed to an extent few had dreamed possible.

Yet in spite of the concern, DDT (along with other persistent chlorinated hydrocarbons, such as dieldrin and aldrin) continued to be used as a pesticide for many a long year. The Department of Agriculture, farmers, business people, and others who might have shared the immediate profits resisted the attempts to ban DDT and the other hazardous pesticides.

One of the great dangers many potent pesticides share with DDT is the fact that they do not break down rapidly. In a fifteen-year period, only half of any given amount of these pesticides will be destroyed and absorbed. In the meantime, the pesticides are available for cattle to eat with grass. Birds take in pesticides through seeds and insects. Fish absorb them from streams and ponds where they are carried by the runoff of rainwater and spraying.

Pesticides accumulate in the fats of animals, which are in turn eaten by other animals higher in the food chain, and on up to human beings, who also store pesticides in their tissues. Even the placenta provides no barrier to DDT and the other similar pesticides. DDT has been found in the tissues of premature and full-term babies, and undoubtedly its molecules are present even in the ovum. In the early 1970s, the high DDT content of mother's milk was a cause of great concern.

The battle over DDT was just the beginning.

DDT, aldrin, and dieldrin are not the only pesticides or contaminants which build up within animal and human bodies. We are all familiar with the Love Canal disaster in upstate New York. Unsafe dumps for toxic wastes are located too near the centers of population all across the country. It is almost impossible to escape the hazards. Waterways, homes, and whole regions have been intolerably contaminated.

If you want more to worry about, consider the long-term dangers of any number of pollutants:

- Herbicides (or weed-killers) that are used by farmers and states pose yet another threat. In 1970, one of these, 2,4,5-T, which kills plants by causing them to overgrow rapidly, was found to cause chromosomal changes in mammals. It was banned for home use, and stores stopped selling it.
  Yet all these years later, you wouldn't have much trouble finding it still in use.

- That isn't all. Diluted 2,4,5-T runs off with rain into lakes and streams and there it contributes to the overgrowth of algae (without killing it). The algae choke the waters and threaten to turn the clear pure waters into nothing but swamps.

- Mercury is used to treat seeds against fungus, and it is discharged into rivers from the manufacturing companies. It's another insidious poison. Swordfish now contains such large amounts of mercury that from most sources it is generally considered unsafe for human consumption.

- Large quantities of chemical fertilizer—nitrates—can enter the water supplies in large enough amounts to pose a real danger to infants.

- Lead poisoning continues to be a concern as people rehabilitate old houses. Many of these layers of paint scraped off the old woodwork contain lead. Tiny fingers can pop flecks into little mouths with no one aware of what is happening. The first sign of trouble could be convulsions. Reportedly one factor that led to the decline of ancient Rome was pervasive lead poisoning from the bottling of Roman wine.

- Now the very air we breath contains pollutants. And acid rain falls many miles from the source of the pollution. Think about the problems with the disposal of nuclear wastes and

113

the safety of nuclear power plants, and shudder. These dangers are not entirely new. For years, researchers have found strontium 90 contamination in milk supplies all over the country, including infant formula supplies.

- The unintentional contaminants are bad enough. Yet over 5,000 intentional additives have entered the food supply. These are the preservatives, the artificial colors, the emulsifiers. Not all of them are risky, but of the 5,000 a bad many are questionable, and it is nearly impossible to avoid them.

- Even a product added to infant formula and canned milk has come under suspicion. Carrageenan, a natural product derived from Irish moss, is an additive that prevents separation in canned formula, canned milk, and other milk products. Carrageenan has been used in infant formula for a quarter of a century, and there have been no reports of harmful effects on human infants. Still, studies do show that degraded carrageenan can cause ulcers in the colons of rabbits and guinea pigs, and some authorities worry about a subtle, yet unknown risk to human beings.

- Natural substances can be as much of a worry as the unnatural additives. Excessive amounts of vitamins in completely natural forms can be toxic—fat-soluble vitamins A and D, to be specific. One meal of polar bear liver could poison an adult just because of the vitamin content. Of course, polar bear liver is not a real danger to most of us. But excessive emphasis on any one food or megavitamin supplement certainly does present a live risk. Twin baby boys, for instance, dined on chicken livers every day—and were nearly poisoned as a result. Fortunately, they survived without permanent damage. But diet extremes, however well meant, can be dangerous.

We cannot worry over all the dangers until we are unable to act against any one of them in an effective and logical way. We cannot go around in space suits, even though for a few especially susceptible children, that has had to be the answer.

The only good solution to the problem seems impossible when looked at in general terms: somehow to eliminate all these contaminants from our environment.

But we can take some action. We are not helpless against the onslaught. We can begin with simple, plain moves like feeding the baby in the best possible way. Good nutrition is protective. Good nutrition builds resistance to whatever the next unknown environmental threat might be.

If you are breastfeeding, remember that another diet for the baby is unlikely to be any safer than human milk, or any nearer purity, and the positive advantages of breastfeeding outweigh the possible contaminants that could enter human milk.

Indeed, because of the inaccuracies of the measuring devices, it is uncertain whether much human milk actually contains substantially more contamination than cow's milk or formula. It is a subtle risk at most.

Recommendations made by Charles F. Wurster in his article "DDT in Mother's Milk" in the *Saturday Review* for May 2, 1970, are still pertinent. Here are some of the precautions he and others have suggested that nursing mothers take to guard against DDT contamination in their milk:

1. Keep away from pesticides, toxic wastes, and other contaminants, insofar as possible.
2. Cut down on the amount of fatty meats and fish you eat.
3. Avoid tobacco smoke.
4. Avoid weight loss while nursing, since the loss of fat could release fat-soluble toxins into the bloodstream.
5. Avoid clothing that has been permanently mothproofed or treated with other chemicals.

If they are available, buy vegetables and fruits that have not been sprayed or treated with chemical fertilizers. Pick out the duller-looking vegetables and fruits since they will not have been polished with hydrocarbons, which in large quantities could be carcinogenic.

Let your grocer know that you want unsprayed and uncontaminated produce, whole-grain flours, less refining in foods, fewer layers of plastic and paper packaging around everything.

Think about growing some of your own produce organically. Home-grown vegetables are safer, and they taste far better than store-bought produce. Even a tiny garden or a windowbox can grow a surprising amount of food and save you some money besides. Grow parsley—a rich source of vitamin C—on your windowsill. Or put some tomato plants in a container on the doorstep.

Or try growing your own sprouts: alfalfa, mung bean, soybean, wheat. They are a fresh source of vitamins and minerals all year round.

As much as possible, in short, prepare your baby's food with the smallest amount of contamination by using wholesome, organically-grown, fresh or fresh-frozen produce.

Be sure also to check on the nitrate and salt content of your water supply before you begin preparing formula and baby foods with tap water. The local health department ought to have the information you need. Or send a sample of your drinking water to the state laboratory or nearest land-grant college for analysis. The fee, if any, is nominal.

If the nitrate content is more than 45 parts per million and you are not breastfeeding, get a pure bottled water for formula-making or use ready-to-feed formula. Use bottled fruit juice or pure bottled water for preparing other drink and food for the baby.

Meanwhile, join the fight to improve the environment. Carry out whatever anti-pollution measures you can privately: recycle your trash; use phosphate- and nitrogen-free laundry preparations (even if you do have to keep them away from children); avoid private use of pesticides and chemical fertilizers.

Cut down on energy consumption. The United States is the ultimate consumer. You have probably heard the often repeated statistic that although we have less than 6 percent of the world's population, we consume 33 percent of the world's energy resources.

Get in touch with your government representatives to support bills that do more than just pay lip service to environmental improvements and wildlife preservation. Think about joining and really working for an ecology or a consumer group.

You are helping to slow the depletion of the world's resources if you breastfeed, if you eat fewer processed foods, if you refrain from using disposable diapers and disposable bottles, if you do a quality job of rearing a small family instead of a quantity job on more children than the world can support.

We must all make every effort, along and with others, to make the future of our children all that we want it to be, long beyond baby foods.

PART
TWO

RECIPES

ABOUT THE RECIPES

In most of the recipes, we have indicated a starting age. These starting ages are approximate. You need to take into account what foods your baby has been introduced to. Use discretion in starting foods at an earlier age than that designated.

Foods containing eggs should not be used until after the baby has been introduced to eggs. Until your baby has been introduced to whole eggs, recipes made with whole eggs can usually be made with yolks only. Use one yolk in place of one whole egg in most recipes; substitute two yolks in "eggy" dishes such as custard.

Use light corn syrup as a sweetener in uncooked foods rather than honey until late in the first year—when you use any sweetener at all. This is a precaution in view of the few reported cases of botulism in young infants fed formula or fruits sweetened with raw honey.

Simple plain vegetables, fruits, and meat purées have no starting age indicated. Use these beginner's foods as appropriate to your child.

Ingredients listed in parentheses are optional either because they are flavorings or because they are foods that may not have been added to the baby's diet or, in the case of salt, may be omitted to keep the salt intake down.

We give metric equivalents because many American households are converting to the metric system of measurements. These

119

equivalents are not exact translations. Instead, each recipe is fixed to correspond to metric measuring utensils. This is for the convenience of the cook—a first priority when we know that the cook has other responsibilities on her mind—like her baby!

SECTION 1:

FRUITS AND FRUIT JUICES

Fruits retain more nutrients if served raw. Since the skin is high in vitamin content, pare fruits very thinly. Cooked fruits retain more nutrients if cooked in their skins and then strained through a sieve or food mill. Apples are especially desirable in that they are digestible and unlikely to cause allergy.

FRUIT PURÉE

Blend sliced, fresh ripe fruits or berries until smooth. If sweetening is desired, add light corn syrup or honey sparingly. Two or more fruits may be blended together.

If you have no blender, mash fully ripe, soft fruits and force them through a sieve or food mill. Fruits such as apple may be scraped with a paring knife to create small shreds that can be sieved.

Fruits, including dried fruits, can also be cooked until soft, then mashed and strained through a sieve or food mill. This is an excellent way to make applesauce.

Use water very sparingly.

FRESH APPLESAUCE
WITH PINEAPPLE

½ cup (125 ml.) pineapple juice
   (100 percent pure unsweetened)
2 large or 4 small apples, cored
   and coarsely cut

Put the pineapple juice in the container of a blender with ½ cup (125 ml.) apple pieces and cover. Blend on high speed. Uncover, and add remaining apple gradually while blending.

FRUIT DRINKS

1. Blend seeded watermelon chunks until liquefied.
2. Blend 1 cup (250 ml.) orange juice with ½ cup (125 ml.) of any other fruit. Sweeten sparingly with honey if desired.
3. Blend 1 cup (250 ml.) apple juice with ½ cup (125 ml.) fruit.
4. For lemonade, blend 2 tablespoons (30 ml.) lemon juice, 1 cup (250 ml.) water, and 1½ tablespoons (22 ml.) honey.

When making your own pure fruit juices with squeezed oranges, grapefruits, or lemons, be sure to strain out the seeds and bits of pulp.

FRUIT PUNCH

Combine dried fruit with orange, pineapple, apple, or grape juice or any combination of these. Unsweetened grapefruit juice may be added for more flavor. Blend on high speed. Taste test your mixture as you go along.

CARROT-PINEAPPLE DRINK

Blend cut-up carrots with unsweetened pineapple juice. Add cracked ice cubes and blend at highest speed.

PINEAPPLE-RHUBARB DRINK

(For people over 9 months old)

Blend raw rhubarb, unsweetened pineapple juice, and honey (if desired) to taste. Add cracked ice cubes, and blend at highest speed.

SECTION 2:
VEGETABLES

Use either fresh or fresh-frozen vegetables, cooked without salt, for babies under nine months old. If you do use canned vegetables, use those canned without salt. Vegetables may be baked, steamed, or stir-fried in just enough vegetable oil to prevent sticking. Or cook them in a small amount of water. In order to prevent loss of vitamins and minerals, do not overcook the vegetables or use too much water.

PURÉED VEGETABLES

Add about ½ cup (125 ml.) liquid to cover the blade of the blender, using water, milk, broth, tomato juice, or vegetable liquid. Add the vegetables gradually while blending on high speed.

If you have no blender, most soft-cooked vegetables, such as carrots, green beans, peas, squash, or sweet potatoes, can be mashed and forced through a sieve or food mill.

Note: Any vegetables from the family meal can be puréed and frozen in cubes to give a real variety and choice when it comes time to make a complete dinner.

TOMATOES

When tomatoes are plentiful and cheap, you can prepare your own tomato juice, tomato soup, and tomato sauce for later use. Your own juices, soups, and sauces will not contain any extra starch or salt. This is also a good way to use up tomatoes that begin to overripen.

Wash the tomatoes, quarter them, and put them in a heavy pan on moderately low heat, mashing them down slightly. Cover and cook, stirring occasionally, until tender.

TOMATO JUICE

(For people over 9 months old)
Pour the cooked tomatoes (see above) into a sieve, letting the juice run through. Do not push down or attempt to purée. The juice will be thin, and a baby will be able to drink it easily.

TOMATO PURÉE

(For people over 9 months old)
Put the pulp remaining from the juice you have prepared into the food mill. Purée until all that is left is the skin and stem end. You may freeze the purée, covered, in ice cube trays. Place the frozen cubes in plastic bags, then seal them and return them to the freezer.

These cubes may be used as the base for a combination dinner prepared from extra ground beef, a little natural cheese, and leftover macaroni—or another nutritious combination of leftovers for a baby dinner.

CREAM OF TOMATO SOUP

(For people over 12 months old)
Add an equal amount of milk to the desired amount of tomato purée. Heat to serving temperature.

For older people, you might add lemon juice or a dash of Worcestershire sauce.

125

WHIPPED MASHED POTATOES

Boil or steam the desired number of scrubbed potatoes until tender. It takes less time if you cut the potatoes into small pieces before cooking.

Retain the cooking water. Remove the skins from the potatoes. (The skins will peel off easily after cooking, and more nutrients will be retained.)

Add milk (or formula) to the potato water, half as much milk as there is water. Mash the potatoes, or put them through a ricer, and return them to the pot with the milk. Using a beater or a wire whisk, whip until smooth and fluffy. You might add more milk, cream, or formula to make them softer or to improve the taste.

Variations
Whipped potatoes can be put through a cookie press or cake decorator to form attractive shapes. Run the shaped potatoes under the broiler to brown slightly.

In the Christmas season, your child may enjoy mashed potato mixed with puréed peas, beans, or spinach, put through a Christmas tree shape in the cookie press, browned under the broiler, and sprinkled with paprika.

VEGETABLE TIMBALES

(For people over 9 months old, 4 servings)

¾ cup (180 ml.) whole milk or
   formula
1 tablespoon (15 ml.) butter or
   margarine
2 eggs or egg yolks

¾ cup (180 ml.) strained,
   chopped, or blended vegetables
(Parsley)
(Grated onion)
(½ teaspoon or 2 ml. salt)

Combine milk, butter or margarine, eggs or yolks, vegetables (and parsley, grated onion, and salt). Pour into buttered custard cups or muffin tins. Place in a pan of hot water. Bake at 350° for about 50 minutes, or until set, when a knife blade inserted comes out clean.

BAKED CORN

(For people over 9 months old, 3 servings)

1 cup (250 ml.) corn, scraped
   from cob, or canned cream-style
   corn
1 egg or egg yolk

2 tablespoons (30 ml.) sweet
   pepper, chopped
(3 tablespoons or 45 ml. onion)
(¼ teaspoon or 1 ml. salt)

Place corn, egg or yolk, sweet pepper (and onion and salt) in blender. Cover and blend to desired consistency. Pour into a buttered baking dish. Bake at 325° for 45 minutes, or until set.

SECTION 3:

MEATS, POULTRY, AND FISH

BLENDER PREPARATION OF MEAT OR FISH

(For people under 9 months old)

1. Cook meat or fish until well done and tender.

2. Do not add salt until baby's portion has been removed.

3. Remove fat and gristle from meat, and skin and bones from fish.

4. Put enough liquid in the container of a blender to cover the blades. (This may be liquid in which meat or fish has cooked, liquid left over from cooking vegetables which are a part of the baby's diet, or water.)

5. Cut the meat or fish, across the grain, thinly, dice, and add to the liquid.

6. Blend to desired consistency—puréed for young babies, chopped for older babies.

LIVER

You ought to serve liver once a week. A word of caution, however: Because chicken liver is so easy to prepare, some mothers have used it more often. But because of its high vitamin A content, it should not be used on a daily basis. Infants have developed vitamin A toxicity from being fed up to ½ cup (120 ml.) chicken liver daily.

1. Chicken, turkey, other poultry—these may be offered at special prices, or you may use the liver from a whole bird which you have purchased.
2. Calf liver—very expensive
3. Beef liver—inexpensive
4. Pork liver—least expensive and very nutritious

BRAISED CHICKEN LIVER

(1 small serving)

¼ to ½ cup (60 to 120 ml.) water
  or vegetable cooking liquid
1 chicken liver

Put enough water or other liquid in a small saucepan to cover the bottom. Add the chicken liver and bring to a boil over moderate heat. Cover and simmer until cooked through (5 to 8 minutes for a small broiler liver).

Remove any connective tissue from liver. Liver and cooking liquid may be blended, mashed, or chopped fine, depending on baby's age.

Babies who dislike liver will frequently eat it when it is prepared as:

LIVER AND POTATO LOAF

(Any number of servings and a good use of leftovers)

1 piece cooked liver
Vegetable cooking liquid or water

Enough soft mashed potatoes
(prepared without salt) to equal
the amount of liver

Remove connective tissue from liver. Blend in the vegetable cooking liquid or put through the fine blade of a food grinder (for older babies). Add soft mashed potato.

Heat through in a 350° oven in a small loaf pan, or heat it in a dish set in water in a covered saucepan on the top of the stove.

Variations

For extra nourishment for older babies, add a beaten egg yolk or whole egg.

Or make it a complete dinner by adding mashed carrots or other soft-cooked and mashed vegetables.

As baby grows older, try adding braised celery, sweet peppers, boiled onions, or parsley.

LIVER AND TOMATOES

(For people over 9 months old, 4 to 6 adult-sized servings)

1 pound (500 g.) calf, beef, or
pork liver, sliced
1 1-pound can (500 g.) tomatoes,
or 3 large fresh tomatoes, peeled
(Pinch of dried basil)

(¼ teaspoon or 1 ml. dried
oregano)
(½ teaspooon or 2 ml. salt)

Put the liver and tomatoes (and basil, oregano, and salt) in a covered casserole dish. Bake in a 350° oven for 50 minutes. Or simmer the liver and tomatoes (and basil, oregano, and salt) in a covered skillet on top of the stove over low heat for 30 to 40 minutes, or until tender. Remove the baby's portion. (You may wish to season the adults' portion at this time.) Remove the

130

connective tissue. Cut up the baby's portion and blend or chop with some cooking liquid to the right consistency for the baby's age and ability.

Variations

For older babies, children, and adults, add 4 chopped small onions, 2 or 3 carrots, 2 sliced celery sticks.

To increase the vitamin C content, add fresh minced parsley or chopped green pepper.

BEEF AND LIVER LOAF

(For people over 9 months old, 8 adult-sized servings)

¾ pound (375 g.) liver
(1 medium onion)
1½ pounds (750 g.) ground beef
⅔ cup (160 ml.) uncooked rolled oats

1 cup (250 ml.) undiluted tomato juice
1 egg or egg yolk
(½ teaspoon or 2 ml. salt)

Put the raw liver (and onion) through a food grinder or purée it in a blender. Mix the liver (and onion) thoroughly with the ground beef, rolled oats, tomato juice , and egg or egg yolk (and salt). Form into a loaf in a greased medium-sized loaf pan. Bake at 350° for 1 hour.

This is a good way to introduce liver to people who think they don't like it.

KIDNEYS

In sections of the country where kidneys are not usually eaten, your butcher may even give them to you. Kidneys are high in nutrients, easily digestible, and low in price. Lamb and veal kidneys are mild and flavorful.

To prepare kidneys, remove the outer membrane, split, and remove the tubules. Beef kidneys can be soaked for half an hour in water to cover as a way of giving them a milder flavor.

BRAISED LAMB KIDNEY

(1 large serving)

Put enough water in a small saucepan to cover the bottom. Add 1 cut-up kidney. Bring to a boil over moderate heat. Cover, lower the heat, and simmer until tender. Blend or chop the kidney with the cooking juices.

BEEF AND KIDNEY LOAF

(For people over 9 months old, 8 adult-sized servings)

For the liver in the *Beef and Liver Loaf* recipe, substitute 4 lamb kidneys or 1 veal kidney. Then cook according to the same directions.

BEEF AND KIDNEY STEW

(For people over 9 months old)

Substitute kidney for one-fourth of the beef in your usual beef stew recipe. Season the stew only after the baby's portion is removed or allow an older baby to have the same seasoning as the older people do.

Blend or chop the baby's portion according to age and ability.

HEART

(5 or 6 servings)

Remove the fat, gristle, and blood vessels from the heart, and cut into cubes. Simmer in stock or water to cover until tender (1 hour or more). Cut up the baby's portion and blend or chop with some cooking liquid. Vegetables may be added as desired.

TONGUE

Tongue is another relatively inexpensive meat which is quite versatile and flavorful. It makes a delicious sandwich spread if blended or ground with a little cooking liquid (and mustard or other seasoning to taste, for older people).

TONGUE

(10 servings)

Cover the tongue with water, and simmer until tender. Remove the skin. A large portion of fresh tongue may have a couple of tiny bones to remove from the back. Blend or chop the baby's portion.

Tongue may be served hot or cold.

SWEETBREADS

Sweetbreads (the pancreas) are a nutritious organ meat. They must be used within a day or two as they do not keep well.

133

BRAISED SWEETBREADS

(2 or 3 servings)

1 pair sweetbreads
½ cup (125 ml.) water

1 tablespoon (15 ml.) vinegar, or
2 tablespoons (30 ml.) lemon
juice

Put the sweetbreads, water, and vinegar in a small saucepan. Bring to a boil over moderate heat. Lower the heat and simmer for 15 minutes. Remove membranes; dice and blend baby's portion in the cooking liquid.

SWEETBREADS IN CREAM SAUCE

(For people over 9 months old, 2 or 3 servings)

3 tablespoons (45 ml.) butter or
oil
3 tablespoons (45 ml.) unbleached,
enriched all-purpose flour
1 cup (250 ml.) milk

Liquid from braising sweetbreads
(1 teaspoon or 5 ml. salt)
(Pinch pepper)
1 pair sweetbreads, braised as
above

Melt the butter or heat oil in a saucepan. Remove from the heat and sprinkle the flour on the butter or oil, stirring in until smooth. Return to the heat. Slowly pour in the combined milk and sweetbreads' cooking liquid, stirring constantly. Simmer while stirring until thickened. (Add seasonings after the baby's portion is removed.)

Add braised sweetbreads. Serve with toast. Baby's portion may be blended with the cream sauce.

Variations
Add 1 tablespoon (15 ml.) chopped pimientos, 1 tablespoon (15 ml.) chopped green pepper, and 1 tablespoon (15 ml.) finely chopped onion to the butter in the portions for people over 9 months old. Sauté until these are tender but not brown, and continue with the recipe, as above.

BRAINS

Brains may be prepared in the same way as sweetbreads. Be sure to simmer them very slowly. You may combine the brains and sweetbreads in the same recipes, if desired.

MEAT OR FISH PIE

(Any number of servings)

Leftover beef, lamb, veal, chicken, organ meats, or fish (Plan on ½ cup or 125 ml. meat, chopped, for each serving.)

Whipped mashed potatoes (see p. 126)

Blend, grind, or chop cooked leftover beef, lamb, veal, chicken, organ meats, or fish in cooking liquid or gravy. Put in pie plate or casserole or individual ovenproof dishes, depending on the number of servings you wish to make.

Top with whipped mashed potatoes. Bake at 350° until heated through, 15 to 20 minutes for individual servings, 45 minutes for large amounts.

Variations
Add any combinations of carrots, peas, chopped celery, chopped green pepper, or parsley.

Spinach or other cooked greens may be blended with the mashed potatoes for a color as well as a taste treat. For older people's portions, you could sprinkle some paprika on top.

FISH LOAF

(For people over 9 months old, 4 medium-sized servings)

2 cups (500 ml.) flaked, cooked
  fish, such as a 1-pound (500 g.)
  can of salmon or 2 7-ounce (210
  g.) cans of tuna or other fish
1½ cups (375 ml.) whole wheat
  bread crumbs

(1 tablespoon or 15 ml. chopped
  onion)
1 beaten egg or egg yolk
½ cup (125 ml.) milk
(½ teaspoon or 2 ml. salt)

Combine fish and crumbs (and onion). Beat together the egg and
milk (and salt). Combine with the fish mixture. Pour into a small
oiled loaf pan, or shape into a small loaf in a larger pan or on a
baking sheet. Bake in a 350° oven for about 30 minutes.

KEDGEREE

(For people over 9 months old, 5 to 6 servings)

3 tablespoons (45 ml.) butter
2 cups (500 ml.) flaked, cooked
  whitefish
2 cups (500 ml.) cooked brown
  rice (or enriched converted rice)

2 hard-cooked eggs, chopped, or
  hard-cooked egg yolks
(½ teaspoon or 2 ml. salt)
(Pinch of pepper)

Melt the butter in a saucepan. Combine the fish, rice, and eggs
(and salt and pepper) and add to the saucepan. Stir over moderate
heat until hot.

IRISH STEW

(For people over 9 months old, 4 to 6 servings)

1 pound (500 g.) lamb breast or
  neck
1 pound (500 g.) potatoes, pared
  and sliced
(1 large onion, sliced)

(½ teaspoon or 2 ml. salt)
(Pinch of ground pepper)
Water
Parsley

Cut the meat into small cubes, ½- to 1-inch (1- to 2-cm.), removing any fat or gristle. Using a 1½-quart (1.5 liters) baking dish or Dutch oven, place a layer of meat in the bottom. Add a layer of potatoes (and a layer of onions). (Season with salt and pepper.) Repeat the layers. Add enough water to come three quarters of the way up the dish. Cover and bake in a moderate oven, 325° for 2 hours or until the meat is tender. Sprinkle with parsley and serve.

Blend or chop the baby's portion, as needed.

COMBINATION DINNERS AND SOUPS

CREAM SOUP

Almost any vegetable including lettuce can be used to prepare cream soups. You may use flour, potato, cornstarch, or egg for thickening, as well as dehydrated or leftover mashed potatoes. The liquid base for a cream soup may be water and milk, broth and milk, vegetable liquid and milk, or, if necessary, the milk may be omitted. You may add additional nonfat dry milk powder and/or wheat germ if you wish to increase the nutritive value.

BASIC CREAM SOUP

(For people over 9 months old, 4 servings)

1 cup (250 ml.) cooked, cut up
  vegetables
½ cup (125 ml.) cooked potato
1½ cups (375 ml.) chicken broth
  or other liquid

¾ cup (185 ml.) milk
(seasonings as desired: salt,
  pepper, onion, parsley)

Put the vegetables, potato, broth or other liquid, and milk (and seasonings) in the container of a blender. Cover and blend until smooth. Heat over boiling water to serving temperature.

If you have no blender, gradually stir 1½ cups (375 ml.) chicken broth or other liquid into ¾ cup (185 ml.) mashed potato. Add 1 cup (250 ml.) cooked strained vegetables (and seasonings). Add ¾ cup (185 ml.) milk and heat over moderate heat to serving temperature, stirring frequently.

To use flour or cornstarch for thickening in cream soup, proceed as for the basic (thin) cream sauce, adding liquid, milk, and puréed vegetables (and seasonings), stirring constantly.

HEALTH SOUP

(For people over 9 months old, any number of servings)

Prepare a stock by simmering together, for 3 to 4 hours, marrow bones, chicken bones, or any other leftover or fresh bones in water and/or vegetable liquid to cover. (Salt, bay leaf, basil, cloves, onion may be added for seasoning along with ¼ cup or 60 ml. vinegar or some tomato juice.)

Strain the stock. Pick any meat from the bones and add it to the stock. Use any combination of fresh, frozen, or canned vegetables, including green beans, tomatoes, potatoes, turnips, parsnips, zucchini, spinach, Swiss chard or other greens, carrots, beets, parsley, green pepper, barley, lentils, chick-peas, cabbage, lima or other shell beans, macaroni, rice, or what have you. Be sure you add only those vegetables that are already on your baby's diet.

Cook for 1½ hours after adding barley, lentils, chick-peas, lima beans, or rice. Add additional water as necessary. Also remember that dried vegetables and grains swell with water as they cook, so small amounts go a long way. Add fresh vegetables according to the time needed to cook them, or stir-fry them in a little oil, adding to the soup just prior to serving.

If you plan to blend this soup for a younger baby, add the vegetables that are not on the baby's diet after the baby's portion has been removed.

This soup may be frozen for later use and reheated as desired.

PEANUT BUTTER SOUP

(For people over 9 months old, 4 servings)

2 tablespoons (30 ml.) butter or
  margarine
(2 tablespoons or 30 ml. chopped
  onion)
1 tablespoon (15 ml.) unbleached
  enriched all-purpose flour

¼ cup (60 ml.) peanut butter
2 cups (500 ml.) whole or
  liquefied dry milk
(Salt and pepper to taste)

Melt the butter in a heavy saucepan. (If the onions are used, sauté them in the butter or margarine until they are transparent.) Remove the pan from the heat and blend in flour and peanut butter. Return to the heat and slowly stir in the milk. (Add salt and pepper.) Continue heating to boiling, stirring constantly.

Children who like peanut butter will probably like this soup.

FISH CHOWDER

(For people over 9 months old, 6 servings)

1 cup (250 ml.) diced potatoes
½ cup (125 ml.) carrots
(1 tablespoon or 15 ml. chopped
  onion)
(2 tablespoons, or 30 ml. diced
  salt pork)
½ pound (250 g.) or 2 cups (500
  ml.) flaked, cooked fish

½ cup (125 ml.) nonfat dry milk
  powder
2 cups (500 ml.) liquid from
  cooking vegetables or fish, plus
  water or milk to make the
  measure

Cook the potatoes and carrots (and onion) in water until tender. (Fry the salt pork until crisp, and add to the vegetables.) Add the fish to the vegetables. Add the dry milk powder to the liquid, stirring until smooth. Combine with the other ingredients. Heat to serving temperature.

Variation
Use minced clams in place of the fish.

(For people over 9 months old)

Combine leftovers or small portions from the family dinner. Chop or process some of these combinations. Do not purée—allow the meal to retain some of its original texture.

1. ½ cup (125 ml.) cubed beef or other cooked meat
   ½ cup (125 ml.) cooked and cubed or mashed vegetable
   ¼ cup (60 ml.) milk

2. ½ cup (125 ml.) cottage cheese
   ⅓ cup (80 ml.) raw fruit
   ¼ cup (60 ml.) cooked cereal

3. ¼ cup (60 ml.) cubed beef or other cooked meat
   2 tablespoons (30 ml.) diced natural mild cheese
   ¼ cup (60 ml.) peeled tomato, or 1 thawed cube of tomato purée
   ¼ cup (60 ml.) cooked macaroni
   ¼ cup (60 ml.) milk

4. ¼ cup (60 ml.) cooked diced chicken
   ½ cup (125 ml.) cream soup
   ¼ cup (60 ml.) cooked noodles

Each of these dinners should be heated over hot water or in a 350° oven.

TUNA AND EGG CASSEROLE

(For people over 9 months old, 2 to 4 servings)

1 7-ounce can (220 g.)
 water-packed tuna
1 tablespoon (15 ml.) lemon juice
1 hard-cooked egg or egg yolk,
 sliced
½ cup (125 ml.) cooked peas
2 tablespoons (30 ml.) butter or
 margarine
1 tablespoon (15 ml.) unbleached
 enriched all-purpose flour

1 cup (250 ml.) milk
½ cup (125 ml.) grated Cheddar
 cheese
(Salt and pepper)
½ cup (125 ml.) buttered fresh
 whole wheat bread crumbs (can
 be prepared easily in the
 blender)

Drain the tuna, flake it, and add lemon juice. Arrange tuna, egg, and peas in alternate layers in a buttered casserole. Melt the butter or margarine and blend with the flour. Add the milk and cheese (and seasonings). Cook, stirring, until thickened. Pour into casserole and top with crumbs. Bake at 400° until brown, about 20 minutes. This may be frozen before baking in individual casseroles, thawed, and heated later.

Variation
Replace tuna with canned salmon or with cooked and diced chicken.

SECTION 5:
CEREALS

Buy natural oats, wheats, or farina. Or use the package directions to prepare cream of wheat, cream of farina, or cream of rice. Although these are enriched and contain added B vitamins, many of the trace minerals are lost in the milling process. Cream of wheat does have wheat germ replaced, however.

You can enrich any cooked cereal by adding 1 tablespoon (15 ml.) per serving of nutritional (or brewer's) yeast, which is ordinarily available in drugstores.

Use whole milk or reconstituted nonfat dry milk to replace any portion or all of the water in cooked cereals. You will need to use a little more milk in place of the water called for. For a younger baby who is not yet on whole milk, use formula or mother's milk.

Here are some other suggestions for improving the value and taste of cooked cereals:

1. Use puréed fruits as sweeteners. Do not use sugar or honey.
2. Raisins, dried fruits, or dried banana flakes may be added while cooking to provide added nourishment and sweetening.
3. Wheat germ, as well as (or in place of) nutritional yeast may be added to increase the nutritive value of the cooked cereal.
4. Instant cereals may have additives to decrease their cooking time, so buy regular cereal if you can. Regular cereals take only a few minutes more cooking time and no more preparation time.

OATMEAL PORRIDGE

(3 servings)

1 cup (250 ml.) water, or 1¼
  cups (310 ml.) milk
⅓ cup (80 ml.) rolled oats
(Salt)

Combine water or milk and oats (and salt). Cook over moderate heat, stirring occasionally, until the mixture comes to a boil. Lower the heat and simmer for 5 minutes. Cover, remove from the heat and let stand for a few minutes.

CREAM OF OATS

(3 servings)

For a very fine texture, put the measured raw oats in blender and grind fine before adding to the liquid. Use formula or other milk for liquid. Follow cooking instructions for *Oatmeal Porridge*.

CORNMEAL MUSH

(4 to 6 servings)

½ cup (125 ml.) cornmeal
½ cup (125 ml.) cold water
½ cup (125 ml.) nonfat dry milk
  powder

(½ teaspoon or 2 ml. salt)
2 cups (500 ml.) boiling water

Combine the cornmeal, cold water, and dry milk powder (and salt). Gradually add to the water boiling over direct heat in the top of a double boiler. Cook over direct heat for 3 to 6 minutes, stirring constantly. Cook for 15 minutes or longer over hot water, stirring occasionally.

Use whole cornmeal. "Degerminated" cornmeal has the germ, or the heart, of the grain, removed. You may wish to sift whole cornmeal to remove pieces of hull.

Millet may be cooked in the same way as cornmeal.

WHOLE WHEAT CEREAL

(3 servings)

¼ cup (60 ml.) cereal
1 cup (250 ml.) boiling water or
  milk
(¼ teaspoon or 1 ml. salt)

Sprinkle cereal into the boiling water, stirring constantly. Cook for 5 minutes or more to desired consistency. Stir occasionally. Cover and remove from the heat. Let sit for a few minutes, or place over boiling water to continue cooking for 10 to 20 minutes.

For older babies, any of the above cereals may be chilled, sliced, and rolled in wheat germ. Sauté in butter, oil, or margarine. Serve with fruit sauce or honey.

BULGUR CEREAL

(For people over 9 months old, 4 servings)
  Bulgur is a whole wheat cereal product. It can be served with milk and fruit or with butter in place of rice or potato, as well as a breakfast dish.

1 cup (250 ml.) bulgur
2 cups (500 ml.) water
(½ teaspoon or 2 ml. salt)

  Mix bulgur and water (and salt) in a saucepan. Bring to a boil, stir with a fork, cover, lower the heat, and simmer for 15 minutes.

Variation
Substitute converted white rice for the bulgur.

BROWN RICE CEREAL

(1 serving)

2 tablespoons (30 ml.) pulverized
  brown rice (see below)
1½ cups (325 ml.) boiling water
(½ teaspoon or 2 ml. salt)

  Prior to measuring, grind the brown rice in the container of a blender, without added liquid, until it is finely pulverized. Then add slowly to the boiling water, stirring constantly until thickened. Cover and let simmer for 10 minutes or longer, depending on how fine the rice is.

GRANOLA: BREAKFAST
CEREAL OR SNACK

(For people over 10 months old, unless it is blended fine, then it is for people over 9 months old; about 36 servings)

4 cups (1 liter) rolled oats
1 cup (250 ml.) shredded coconut
1 cup (250 ml.) chopped nuts
1 cup (250 ml.) rye or bran
1 cup (250 ml.) roasted soybeans
1 cup (250 ml.) hulled sunflower
  seeds

½ cup (125 ml.) honey, heated
½ cup (125 ml.) corn, peanut,
  wheat germ, soybean, sesame,
  safflower, or sunflower oil
½ teaspoon (2 ml.) vanilla

Mix the oats, coconut, nuts, grain, beans, and seeds. Stir in the hot honey, oil, and vanilla. Mix thoroughly. (You may want to use your fingers.) Spread out on an oiled baking sheet. Bake at 325° for 20 to 30 minutes. You may want to stir after 15 minutes in the oven, so that mixture will brown evenly.

Cool and store in a tightly covered container. Serve plain as a treat, or with milk and fruit as a breakfast cereal.

For young toddlers, put a serving in the container of a blender and grind fine. Add finely chopped fresh or dried fruit as desired. This is very filling!

Variations
The nuts, grains (except oats), and seeds may be varied as desired, using whole wheat flour, sesame seeds, millet, etc. In case of allergy, omit the offending grains.

DRY CEREALS FOR TODDLERS

Shredded Wheat: Dot with butter or margarine. Pour on 2 tablespoons (30 ml.) boiling water or hot milk. Add fruit, honey (if desired), and cold milk.

Prepare other cereals, such as puffed rice, puffed wheat, or Grape Nuts, in the same way.

Toasted wheat germ may be served as a cereal with milk or as a topping for other cereals. To toast raw wheat germ, place on baking sheet and bake in a 325° oven for 10 to 15 minutes, stirring occasionally. Store in an airtight jar in a cool place.

Check the ingredients on other dry cereals you may wish to feed your toddler. Most of them contain BHT or large amounts of sugar. If you choose to add a sweetener, at least you have control over the amount.

BREADS AND TEETHING BISCUITS

These recipes utilize the *Cornell Triple-Rich Formula*. Add the formula to any recipe for baked goods. In the bottom of each cup (250 ml.) of flour called for in a recipe, add 1 tablespoon (15 ml.) soy flour, 1 tablespoon (15 ml.) powdered nonfat dry milk (not the instant crystals), and 1 teaspoon (5 ml.) wheat germ. Fill the rest of the measure with whole grain, all-purpose enriched, and unbleached white flour, or other flour.

TEETHING BISCUITS

(For people over 9 months old)

1 egg yolk, beaten
2 tablespoons (30 ml.) honey
2 tablespoons (30 ml.) molasses
2 tablespoons (30 ml.) oil
1 teaspoon (5 ml.) vanilla
¾ cup (185 ml.) whole wheat
   flour

1 tablespoon (15 ml.) soy flour
1 tablespoon (15 ml.) wheat germ
1½ tablespoons (22 ml.) nonfat
   dry milk powder

Blend together the egg yolk, honey, molasses, oil, and vanilla, and mix in the blended whole wheat and soy flours, wheat germ, and dry milk powder. Roll out the dough very thinly, to a thickness of ⅛ to ¼ inch (.25 cm. to .5 cm.). Cut in baby-finger-length rectangles.

Bake at 350° on an ungreased cookie sheet for 15 minutes.

Remove from the sheet and cool thoroughly on wire rack. Store in tightly covered container.

ZWIEBACK

Cut homemade whole grain bread in ½-inch-thick (1-cm.) slices.

Cut the slices in thirds. Bake in a 250° oven for 1 hour, or until dried out and hard like Melba toast.

KENNEBEC TOAST

(This recipe contains no eggs)
(For people over 9 months old)

2 cups (500 ml.) whole wheat or
  sifted unbleached enriched
  all-purpose white flour
4 teaspoons (20 ml.) baking
  powder

¾ teaspoon (3 ml.) salt
3 tablespoons (45 ml.) butter or
  margarine
About ¾ cup (185 ml.) milk

Combine flour, baking powder, and salt. Cut in butter or margarine with the dry ingredients. Add milk to make a soft dough. Put dough on a well-floured surface. Fold it lightly two or three times. Roll thin, about ¼- to ½-inch (.5- to 1-cm.) thick and cut in squares.

Bake at 425° on a buttered baking sheet, until brown, about 10 minutes.

While still warm, split squares and spread with butter and hot applesauce or apple butter.

BISCUITS

(This recipe contains no eggs)
(For people over 9 months old)

Make the recipe for *Kennebec Toast*, but pat dough out to ½- to ¾-inch (1- to 1.5-cm.) thickness. Cut in rounds and brush the tops with milk. Bake at 425° on a buttered baking sheet, or in a circle on a cake pan, for about 15 minutes, or until brown

ROLLED OAT BISCUITS

(This recipe contains no wheat, eggs, or milk)
(For people over 9 months old, 10 biscuits)

2 cups (500 ml.) finely ground
  oats
3 teaspoons (15 ml.) baking
  powder
1 teaspoon (5 ml.) salt

3 tablespoons (45 ml.) shortening
6 to 8 tablespoons (90 to 120 ml.)
  water (use milk if no milk
  allergy)

Grind the oats in the container of a blender prior to measuring. Mix with the baking powder and salt. Cut in the shortening. Stir in enough water to make a stiff dough. Pat out and cut into 10 rounds and place on baking sheet.

Bake at 450° for 10 to 12 minutes. Cool on wire racks. Store in a tightly covered container.

BABY'S HEALTH CRACKERS

(This recipe contains no eggs)
(For people over 9 months old)

2½ cups (625 ml.) sifted whole
  wheat flour
2 tablespoons (30 ml.) soy flour
2 tablespoons (30 ml.) nonfat dry
  milk powder
2 teaspoons (10 ml.) wheat germ

3 tablespoons (45 ml.) oil
3 tablespoons (45 ml.) honey
⅔ cup (160 ml.) milk
1 teaspoon (5 ml.) vanilla
(Pinch of salt)

Mix together the whole wheat and soy flours, nonfat dry milk powder, and wheat germ. Combine the oil, honey, milk, and vanilla (and salt). Blend the liquid ingredients with the dry ingredients, and knead until they form a smooth ball. You may need to add water or milk drop by drop in order to achieve a kneadable dough without letting it get too soft. Roll out on a floured surface until as thin as possible. Cut into 1-inch (2-cm.) strips.

Bake at 350° on a greased baking sheet for 8 to 10 minutes, or until brown.

Remove from the baking sheet, cool thoroughly on wire racks, and store in a tightly covered container.

GRAHAM CRACKERS

(This recipe contains no eggs)
(For people over 9 months old)

1 cup (250 ml.) graham or whole wheat flour
1 cup (250 ml.) sifted, unbleached, enriched all-purpose white flour
1 teaspoon (5 ml.) baking powder
(1 teaspoon or 5 ml. salt)
¼ cup (60 ml.) butter or margarine
¼ cup (60 ml.) honey
About ¼ cup (60 ml.) milk

Combine the graham and white flours, and baking powder (and salt). Cut in the butter or margarine until the mixture resembles cornmeal. Stir in the honey. Add enough milk to make a stiff dough. Roll the dough out on a floured surface to a ¼-inch (.5-cm.) thickness. Cut into squares. Prick the surface of the squares with a fork. Brush with milk.

Bake at 400° on an ungreased baking sheet for about 18 minutes, or until golden brown.

These are quite hard and can be used as teething biscuits if rolled slightly thicker and cut in sticks. Cool thoroughly on wire racks before storing in a tightly covered container. The crackers may also be used as crumbs for pie shells.

OATMEAL CRACKERS

(This recipe contains no wheat, eggs, or milk)

4 cups (1 liter) rolled oats
¾ teaspoon (3 ml.) salt
1 cup (250 ml.) water (or milk, if
   no milk allergy)
4 tablespoons (60 ml.) honey or
   light corn syrup

½ cup (125 ml.) oil
1 cup (250 ml.) additional rolled
   oats

Grind the 4 cups (1 liter) oats in blender, 1 cup (250 ml.) at a time. Add the salt. In a bowl, blend the water (or milk), honey, and oil. Add the 4 cups (1 liter) ground oats. This will make a stiff dough. Let sit for a few minutes while you grind another cup of oats to flour the work surface. Turn the dough out onto the oat-floured board and roll very thinly. Cut into squares or rounds. Prick each square or round with a fork. Place on an ungreased baking sheet.

Bake at 350° for about 20 minutes, or until browned. Cool on wire racks, and store in tightly covered containers.

These crackers may be used in place of graham crackers in most recipes calling for graham cracker crumbs.

Note: We have been told of one baby who was allergic to just about everything except mother's milk and oats. She used these crackers as her only form of bread well into the second year.

YEAST BREADS

HINTS ON MAKING YEAST BREAD

When adding lukewarm water to a bread recipe, make sure it is just that. If the water is too hot, it will kill the yeast; if the water, milk, and other ingredients are too cold, the rising action will be retarded.

Knead most breads for about 10 minutes, using a rolling and

punching action with the palms of your hands. The dough will become smoother, more elastic, and less sticky as you knead. To prevent chilling, cover the dough with a clean towel if you are called away even for a moment.

Set the bread to rise, covered with a clean towel, in a warm, draft-free place. The ideal temperature is 80° to 85°. A good spot is an unheated oven with a large pan of hot water on the rack beneath the bread. Do not put the bowl of dough directly on a hot radiator.

FAMILY BREAD

(For people over 9 months old, 2 loaves)

1 package, or 1 tablespoon (15 ml.) dry yeast
1 cup (250 ml.) lukewarm water
2 tablespoons (30 ml.) honey
3 cups (750 ml.) warmed milk
2 tablespoons (30 ml.) salt
2 tablespoons (30 ml.) oil
7 cups (1.75 liters) whole wheat flour

¼ cup (60 ml.) soy flour
¼ cup (60 ml.) nonfat dry milk powder
¼ cup (60 ml.) wheat germ
¼ cup (60 ml.) nutritional or brewer's yeast

Mix the dry yeast, water, and honey, and let stand in a warm place for 45 minutes. Add the warmed milk, salt, and oil. Then mix in the flours, dry milk powder, wheat germ, and nutritional yeast. Knead for 10 minutes, or until the dough is smooth and slightly sticky. Cover and let rise in a warm place for 1 hour.

Punch the dough down with your fist, gather in its edges, and put it on a floured board. Cover and let rest for 10 to 15 minutes. Then shape into loaves, and place in oiled 9- × 5½- × 3-inch (18- × 11- × 6-cm.) pans. Cover and let rise in a warm place for 1 hour.

Bake at 400° for 20 minutes, then at 350° for 30 minutes. Remove from the pans immediately and let cool on wire racks. Butter the crusts while they are still warm.

WHITE BREAD PLUS

(For people over 9 months old)

The following recipe makes 4 loaves of enriched white bread with added nutrients. Plan on about 5 hours from start to finish.

2 cups (500 ml.) milk, scalded (or use buttermilk or sour milk for a softer dough)

4 tablespoons (60 ml.) honey

1½ tablespoons (22 ml.) salt

3 tablespoons (45 ml.) softened butter, margarine, or oil

2 packages dry yeast (2 tablespoons or 30 ml.), or 2 yeast cakes

2 cups (500 ml.) lukewarm water

½ cup (125 ml.) soy flour

½ cup (125 ml.) nonfat dry milk powder

¼ cup (60 ml.) wheat germ

12 cups (3 liters) sifted, unbleached, enriched all-purpose white flour

Combine the milk, honey, salt, and butter, margarine or oil. Stir until dissolved. Let cool to lukewarm. Soften the yeast in ½ cup (125 ml.) of the lukewarm water. Add with the remaining water to the cooled milk mixture.

Add the soy flour, dry milk powder, and wheat germ sifted with about 4 cups (1 liter) of the unbleached white flour. Blend in additional flour until the dough leaves the sides of the bowl.

Use the remaining flour to flour the work surface. Turn the dough out on the floured surface and knead until smooth and elastic, about 10 to 15 minutes.

Place in an oiled or buttered bowl, turning once. Cover closely with dish towel, and let rise in a warm place for about 1½ hours, or until the impression of a finger stays in the dough.

Punch down the dough to release the gas. Cover the dough and let rise for another ½ hour.

Put on a floured surface, flatten, divide, and shape into 4 balls. Cover closely and let rest for 15 minutes. Shape into 4 loaves.

Put in 4 oiled 8- × 5- × 2½-inch (16- × 10- × 5-cm.) loaf pans, or make old-fashioned double loaves (using large loaf tins with 2 balls of dough in each tin). Keep covered in a warm place until the dough fills the pans and the centers rise above the tops of the pans, about 1½ hours.

Bake at 400° for about 40 minutes. Remove from the pans at once and cool on wire racks. Butter the warm crusts if you want a soft crust.

Variation

Use 3 cups (750 ml.) whole wheat flour in place of the same amount of white flour. Bake in a 375° oven.

OATMEAL BREAD

(For people over 9 months old, 2 large loaves)

2 packages dry yeast, or 2 tablespoons (30 ml.) dry yeast
½ cup (125 ml.) warm water
1 tablespoon (15 ml.) honey
1 cup (250 ml.) rolled oats
2 teaspoons (10 ml.) salt
⅓ cup (80 ml.) oil
½ cup (125 ml.) molasses
1½ cups (375 ml.) boiling water

2 eggs, beaten
5 cups (1.25 liters) unbleached, enriched all-purpose white flour
2 tablespoons (30 ml.) soy flour
2 tablespoons (30 ml.) nonfat dry milk powder
1 tablespoon (15 ml.) wheat germ
2 tablespoons (30 ml.) nutritional or brewer's yeast

Dissolve the dry yeast in the lukewarm water and honey. Let stand in a warm place for 45 minutes. Meanwhile, combine the oats, salt, oil, and molasses, and pour the boiling water over this mixture. When the mixture has cooled to lukewarm (so it will not kill the yeast), combine with the yeast mixture, and add the eggs, flours, dry milk powder, wheat germ, and nutritional yeast.

Put the dough on a floured surface and knead for 5 to 8 minutes, or until the dough is smooth and elastic.

Refrigerate for 2 hours. Knead for 1 minute longer on a floured surface. Cover and let stand for 10 minutes, then shape into loaves. Place in 2 oiled 9- × 5½- × 3-inch (18-× 11-× 6-cm.) loaf pans. Cover and let rise in a warm place for 1 hour.

Bake at 350° for 45 minutes. Remove from the pans at once, and let cool on wire racks. Butter the crusts while they are still warm.

ANADAMA BREAD PLUS

(For people over 9 months old, 2 large loaves)

1 cup (250 ml.) scalded milk
1 cup (250 ml.) boiling water
1 cup (250 ml.) yellow
   undegerminated cornmeal
3 tablespoons (45 ml.) butter or
   margarine
½ cup (125 ml.) molasses
2 teaspoons (10 ml.) salt
2 packages dry yeast or 2
   tablespoons (30 ml.) dry yeast

½ cup (125 ml.) lukewarm water
⅓ cup (80 ml.) soy flour
5 to 5½ cups (1.25 to 1.375
   liters) sifted, unbleached,
   enriched all-purpose white flour
⅓ cup (80 ml.) nonfat dry milk
   powder
3 teaspoons (15 ml.) wheat germ

Combine the hot milk and water and slowly add the cornmeal, stirring constantly. Add the butter or margarine, molasses, and salt. Let stand until lukewarm. Sprinkle the yeast over the lukewarm water to dissolve it. Add about 2 cups (500 ml.) of the white flour and the soy flour, dry milk powder, and wheat germ to the cornmeal mixture. Add the dissolved yeast. Add the remaining white flour. Knead on a floured board for 7 minutes, or until the dough is smooth and elastic. Put in an oiled bowl. Turn once to bring the oiled side up. Cover and let rise in a warm place until double in bulk, about 1½ hours. Punch the dough down.

Divide in 2 parts, and shape each into a loaf. Put in 2 oiled 9- × 5- × 3-inch (18- ×   10- × 6-cm.) pans. Cover and let rise in a warm place until double in bulk, about 45 minutes.

Bake at 375° for 40 to 50 minutes. Remove from the pans at once to cool on wire racks. For softer crusts, brush with butter while still warm.

RYE BREAD

(This recipe contains no wheat, eggs, or milk)
(For people over 9 months old, 2 large loaves)

1 package dry yeast, or 1
  tablespoon (15 ml.) dry yeast
1⅓ cups (330 ml.) lukewarm
  water
2 tablespoons (30 ml.) honey or
  light corn syrup

1½ teaspoons (7 ml.) salt
2 tablespoons (30 ml.) melted
  shortening
About 5 cups (1.25 liters) light
  rye flour, sifted

Soak the yeast in the lukewarm water with 1 teaspoon (5 ml.) honey. Let stand for 5 minutes. Add the remaining honey or corn syrup, salt, and melted shortening. Stir in half the flour and beat until smooth.

Add half the remaining flour to the mixture. Sprinkle the rest of the flour on the work surface. Turn the dough out onto the work surface and knead until smooth and elastic. Put the dough in an oiled bowl, cover with a towel, and let rise in a warm place for 1 hour, or until double in bulk. Divide into 2 parts and shape each into a loaf on a floured board. Put in 2 oiled 9- × 5½- × 3-inch (18- × 11- × 6-cm.) loaf pans, and let rise until double, about 1 hour.

Bake at 425° for 15 minutes. Lower the oven temperature to 350° and bake for 30 minutes longer. Remove from the pans at once and let cool on wire racks.

BROWN BREAD

(This recipe contains no eggs)
(For people over 9 months old, 1 large loaf)

This simple bread is highly nutritious. Use a 2-pound (1-kg.) coffee can for a mold. Tie a piece of greased brown paper bag over the top with string. Set in boiling water in a kettle or Dutch oven with a lid that fits.

¾ cup (180 ml.) undegerminated cornmeal
½ cup (125 ml.) whole wheat flour
¼ cup (60 ml.) rye flour
1 teaspoon (5 ml.) baking soda

½ teaspoon (2 ml.) salt
6 tablespoons (90 ml.) molasses
1 cup (250 ml.) sour milk or buttermilk
1 cup (250 ml.) raisins

Combine the cornmeal, wheat and rye flours, baking soda, and salt. Mix together the molasses, milk, and raisins and stir into the dry ingredients. Fill the buttered mold and steam over low heat for 1½ to 2 hours.

Variation
(This recipe contains no wheat or eggs)

Make the above recipe substituting rye flour for the whole wheat flour.

BANANA BREAD

(For people over 9 months old, 1 large loaf)

3 small ripe bananas
¾ cup (180 ml.) honey
¼ cup (60 ml.) melted butter or
  margarine
1 teaspoon (5 ml.) baking soda

½ teaspoon (2 ml.) salt
2 eggs, beaten
1½ cups (375 ml.) whole wheat
  flour

Mash the bananas. Add the honey, butter or margarine, baking soda, salt, eggs, and flour in that order. Mix well. Pour into an oiled 9- × 5½- × 3-inch (18- × 11- × 6-cm.) loaf pan.

Bake at 350° for 1 hour. Remove from the pan at once and cool on a wire rack.

BARLEY QUICK BREAD

(This recipe contains no wheat or eggs)
(For people over 9 months old, one 14-inch [28-cm.] round loaf)

2 cups (500 ml.) barley flour
2 teaspoons (10 ml.) baking
  powder
(¾ teaspoon or 3 ml. salt)
1 cup (250 ml.) undiluted

evaporated milk, or a mixture of
half milk, half cream
1 teaspoon (5 ml.) honey
2 tablespoons (30 ml.) melted
  butter or margarine

Combine the flour and baking powder (and salt). Stir in the evaporated milk, or half-and-half, with the melted butter, or margarine and honey. Stir until smooth. Pour out onto a well-buttered baking sheet, and, with floured hands, pat into a 14-inch (28-cm.) circle, about ½-inch (1-cm.) thick. Prick the surface with a fork, and bake at 400° for 10 minutes, or until lightly browned. Cut in wedges when cool.

Variation
Substitute rye flour for the barley flour.

SECTION 7:

OTHER BAKED GOODS

COOKIES

GINGER COOKIES

(This recipe contains no eggs or milk)
(For people over 9 months old, makes 48 cookies)

This makes a thin, crisp molasses cookie. You can use any leftover cookie crumbs to make a pie shell following the directions for the *Graham Cracker Pie Shell* on pg. 171.

⅓ cup (80 ml.) brown sugar
2 teaspoons (10 ml.) baking soda
1 teaspoon (5 ml.) ground ginger
1 teaspoon (5 ml.) salt
3 cups (750 ml.) unbleached,

enriched all-purpose white flour
or whole wheat flour
1 cup (250 ml.) butter or
margarine
⅔ cup (160 ml.) molasses

Mix and sift together the brown sugar, baking soda, ginger, salt, and flour. Cut in the butter or margarine until the mixture resembles coarse cornmeal. Add the molasses. Knead to blend thoroughly. Chill. Roll thinly on a floured surface and cut with cookie cutters.

Bake at 375° for 8 to 10 minutes, or until lightly browned. Cool thoroughly on wire racks, and store in tightly covered containers.

162

GINGERBREAD MEN

(This recipe contains no eggs)
(For people over 9 months old, 50 large men)
  This makes a soft bread-like cookie, the kind children like.

¾ cup (180 ml.) melted butter or
  margarine
1 cup (250 ml.) molasses
½ cup (125 ml.) honey
1 cup (250 ml.) thick sour milk or
  buttermilk
6½ cups (1.625 liters) whole
  wheat flour or sifted,
  unbleached, enriched all-purpose
  white flour

½ teaspoon (2 ml.) salt
2 teaspoons (10 ml.) ground
  ginger
4 teaspoons (20 ml.) baking
  powder
¾ teaspoon (3 ml.) baking soda
1 tablespoon (15 ml.) lemon or
  orange extract

  Mix together the melted butter or margarine, molasses, and
honey until smooth. Stir in the sour milk or buttermilk, then the
flour, which has been sifted with the salt, ginger, baking powder,
and baking soda. Add the lemon extract. Mix to a smooth stiff
dough. Roll out on a lightly floured surface to ⅓-inch (.75-cm.)
thick. Cut into shapes. Place on an ungreased baking sheet.
  Bake at 350° for 8 to 10 minutes. Cool on wire racks.
  Decorate with bits of preserved fruits and/or raisins, for features
and buttons. The fruits may be placed on the cookies before
baking.

RYE GINGER COOKIES

(This recipe contains no eggs, wheat, or milk)
(For people over 9 months old, about 36 cookies)

¼ cup (60 ml.) margarine that is made without milk
¼ cup (60 ml.) honey
½ cup (125 ml.) blackstrap molasses
1¼ cups (310 ml.) rye flour
1¼ cups (310 ml.) cornstarch
1 teaspoon (5 ml.) baking soda
¼ teaspoon (1 ml.) ground cloves
¾ teaspoon (3 ml.) ground cinnamon
¼ teaspoon (1 ml.) ground ginger
½ teaspoon (2 ml.) salt
½ cup (125 ml.) hot water
(Raisins)

Cream the margarine, honey, and molasses together. Gradually add the rye flour which has been sifted with the cornstarch, baking soda, cloves, cinnamon, ginger, and salt, alternating with the water. (Add the raisins if desired.)

Roll out on a floured surface. If sticky, work in a small amount of flour as necessary. Cut in desired shapes.

Bake at 350° for 8 minutes. Cool on wire racks. Store in a tightly covered container.

CORNMEAL COOKIES

(This recipe contains no wheat or milk)
(For people over 9 months old, 24 to 36 cookies)

⅓ cup (80 ml.) margarine that is made without milk
1 cup (250 ml.) dark brown sugar
1 egg
3 tablespoons (45 ml.) water
2 cups (500 ml.) cornmeal
1 teaspoon (5 ml.) vanilla

Mix together the margarine, brown sugar, and egg. Stir in the water, cornmeal, and vanilla. Drop from a teaspoon onto a greased baking sheet.

Bake at 375° for 15 minutes. Cool on wire racks. Store in a tightly covered container.

HONEY BARLEY OR RICE COOKIES

(This recipe contains no eggs, wheat, or milk)
(For people over 9 months old, 24 cookies)

½ cup (125 ml.) honey
⅓ cup (80 ml.) oil
1 cup (250 ml.) barley or rice
  flour, sifted

½ teaspoon (2 ml.) baking powder
¼ teaspoon (1 ml.) baking soda
¼ teaspoon (1 ml.) salt
½ teaspoon (2 ml.) vanilla

Mix the honey and oil with the flour, baking powder, baking soda, and salt. Add the vanilla. Drop from a teaspoon onto a greased baking sheet.

Bake at 375° for 12 to 15 minutes. Cool on wire racks, and store in a tightly covered container.

SCOTCH FINGERS

(This recipe contains no eggs, wheat, or milk)
(For people over 9 months old, 12 to 18 cookies)

1 cup (250 ml.) rolled oats
¼ teaspoon (1 ml.) salt
1½ teaspoons (7 ml.) baking
  powder
1 tablespoon (15 ml.) honey or
  light corn syrup

2 tablespoons (30 ml.) warm
  water
2 tablespoons (30 ml.) molasses
1 tablespoon (15 ml.) melted
  margarine that is made without
  milk

Before measuring, grind the rolled oats fine in blender. Then mix them with the salt and baking powder. Stir in the honey, warm water, molasses, and melted margarine. Flour a board with additional ground oats. Roll the dough to a very thin sheet. Cut in strips and place on a greased baking sheet.

Bake at 425° for 15 to 20 minutes. Cool on wire racks, and store in a tightly covered container.

Variation
Add ½ teaspoon (2 ml.) ground cloves or ground allspice.

APPLESAUCE CAKE

(This recipe contains no eggs, wheat, or milk)
(For people over 9 months old, 1 8-inch layer)

½ cup (125 ml.) shortening
¾ cup (185 ml.) honey
1½ cups (375 ml.) applesauce
¾ cup (185 ml.) barley flour
½ teaspoon (2 ml.) ground
  cinnamon

½ teaspoon (2 ml.) ground cloves
1 teaspoon (5 ml.) baking soda
¼ teaspoon (1 ml.) salt

Mix together the shortening, honey, and applesauce. Stir in the barley flour, which has been sifted with the cinnamon, cloves, baking soda, and salt.

Pour into an oiled 8-inch (16-cm.) cake pan.

Bake at 350° for 50 minutes. Cool for 10 minutes in the pan, then remove from the pan and finish cooling on wire rack.

JOHNNY CAKE

(This recipe contains no wheat)
(For people over 9 months old, 1 8-inch square cake)

1 cup (250 ml.) cornmeal
½ teaspoon (2 ml.) baking soda
1 teaspoon (5 ml.) cream of tartar
¼ teaspoon (1 ml.) salt
¼ cup (60 ml.) honey

1 cup (250 ml.) milk
1 egg, well beaten
1 tablespoon (15 ml.) melted
  butter or margarine
1 tablespoon (15 ml.) molasses

Sift together the cornmeal, baking soda, cream of tartar, and salt. Combine the honey, milk, egg, butter or margarine, and molasses, and add to the dry ingredients. Pour into an oiled 8-inch (15-cm.) square cake pan. Bake at 425° for 30 minutes. Serve hot.

EGGLESS CAKE

(This recipe contains no eggs)
(For people over 12 months old, 1 9-inch layer)

½ cup (125 ml.) butter or
 margarine
¾ cup (185 ml.) honey
2 cups (500 ml.) sifted,
 unbleached, enriched all-purpose
 white flour
½ teaspoon (2 ml.) baking soda

½ teaspoon (2 ml.) ground cloves
½ teaspoon (2 ml.) ground
 cinnamon
⅛ teaspoon (.5 ml.) salt
½ cup (125 ml.) sour milk or
 buttermilk
(1 cup or 250 ml. chopped raisins)

Cream the butter or margarine with the honey. Add the flour, which has been sifted with the baking soda, cloves, cinnamon, and salt, alternately with the milk. (Beat in raisins if desired.) Pour into a greased and floured 9-inch (18-cm.) cake pan.

Bake at 350° for 45 minutes. Cool for 10 minutes in the pan, then remove from the pan to finish cooling on a wire rack.

FIRST BIRTHDAY CAKE

(For people at 12 months old, 2-layer cake)

1 cup (250 ml.) butter or
 margarine
1½ cups (375 ml.) honey
4 eggs, beaten
2 cups (500 ml.) sifted,
 unbleached, enriched all-purpose
 white flour, with the Cornell
 Triple-Rich Formula (see p.149)

2 teaspoons (10 ml.) baking soda
1 teaspoon (5 ml.) ground
 cinnamon
1 teaspoon (5 ml.) ground ginger
¼ teaspoon (1 ml.) salt
1⅓ cups (320 ml.) sour cream

Cream together the honey and butter. Add the beaten eggs. Add the flour, which has been sifted with the baking soda, cinnamon, ginger, and salt, alternately with the sour cream. Pour into 2 oiled and floured 9-inch (18-cm.) cake pans.

Bake at 350° for 40 minutes. Ice with *Basic Frosting, Honey-Peanut Butter Icing,* or *Ricotta Frosting* (see pp. 168, 169).

GRAHAM CRACKER TORTE

(For people over 12 months old, 2 thin 8-inch layers)

½ cup (125 ml.) butter or
   margarine
½ cup (125 ml.) honey
3 eggs
½ cup (125 ml.) unbleached,
   enriched all-purpose white flour

1½ teaspoons (7 ml.) baking
   powder
1½ cups (375 ml.) fine graham
   cracker crumbs
¾ cup (180 ml.) milk

Beat together thoroughly the butter or margarine, honey, and eggs. Add the flour, which has been sifted with the baking powder and graham cracker crumbs, alternately with the milk. Pour into 2 greased and floured 8-inch (16-cm.) cake pans.

Bake at 350° for 25 minutes. Let cool for 10 minutes in the pans, then turn out on wire racks to finish cooling. Serve with whipped cream or other topping, if desired.

CAKE TOPPINGS

HONEY–PEANUT BUTTER ICING

4 tablespoons (60 ml.) butter or
   margarine
¼ cup (60 ml.) honey

½ cup (125 ml.) finely ground
   peanuts, or ½ cup (125 ml.)
   peanut butter

Bring the butter and honey to a boil. Remove from the heat and blend in the finely ground peanuts. Slip the iced cake under the broiler until lightly toasted.

BASIC FROSTING

(For a 1-layer cake. Double the recipe to cover a 2-layer cake.)

⅔ cup (160 ml.) chilled
  evaporated milk, or ½ cup (125
  ml.) nonfat dry milk powder
  with ½ cup (125 ml.) ice water

1 teaspoon (5 ml.) honey
½ teaspoon (2 ml.) vanilla

Whip the chilled evaporated milk or the nonfat dry milk powder and ice water with the honey and vanilla. You can tint some and squeeze it through a cake decorator onto wax paper to form decorations. Quick-freeze any decorations and add to cake just before serving.

RICOTTA FROSTING

2 cups (500 ml.) ricotta cheese
2 tablespoons (30 ml.) honey
1 teaspoon (5 ml.) vanilla

Blend the ricotta cheese, honey, and vanilla in a blender until smooth, or beat at high speed with an electric mixer. Chill before using as a frosting to keep firm and prevent spoilage.

Variation
(This recipe contains no milk)
  Substitute tofu for the ricotta cheese.

PIE CRUST

Use whole wheat or part whole wheat flour in making pie crust, according to the following rules:

1. Use 1 part shortening to 3 parts flour. Example: Use ⅓ cup (80 ml.) shortening to 1 cup (250 ml.) flour.

2. Use ½ teaspoon (2 ml.) salt for each cup flour.

3. Use ice water or milk to bind the pastry. It takes approximately 2 tablespoons (30 ml.) for each cup of flour.

4. Sift the measured unbleached, enriched all-purpose flour with whole wheat flour, as desired.

5. Cut in shortening with a pastry blender or 2 knives until the mixture resembles cornmeal. If using oil rather than shortening, stir it in thoroughly.

6. Add ice water or cold milk, sprinkling in a tablespoon at a time, mixing as you add it.

7. When the dough forms a ball, remove the desired amount to floured surface. Turn dough over, and, with a floured rolling pin, flatten the dough with a minimum of strokes to avoid toughening. Make 3 horizontal depressions in the dough with the rolling pin, then turn the dough to right angles and make 3 more depressions. Then roll out in short strokes from the center until the size and shape of the crust fits the pan.

If using oil, roll out between two pieces of wax paper. Wet the surface of the counter slightly before laying down the first piece of paper to prevent slipping.

8. Handle the dough as little as possible and use just enough liquid to bind it so it will not be tough. You may omit the liquid entirely when making oil pastry.

To make the rolling easier, chill before rolling.

To make a tender cheese pastry, add ⅓ cup (80 ml.) cottage cheese or cream cheese for each cup (250 ml.) of flour.

For a single-crust pie:
Use 1½ cups (375 ml.) flour. Makes 1 9- to 10-inch (18- to 20-cm.) pie crust.

For a double-crust pie:
Use 2 cups (500 ml.) flour. Makes 2 8- to 9-inch (16- to 18-cm.) pie crusts.
Use 3 cups (750 ml.) flour to make a 10-inch (20-cm.) double-crust pie.

To lessen the caloric impact of pie, use a top crust only on fruit or mince pies.

To make tarts, cut the pastry into squares. Place the filling on half the square (diagonally). Fold the other half over and pinch the edges together with a fork.

For open tarts, cut the pastry into rounds and place in muffin tins. Bake and then fill or pour the filling in the tart first and then bake. Most pies can be adapted to tarts, but will not need to be baked as long. Cut baking time by one-third to one-half.

GRAHAM CRACKER PIE SHELL

¼ cup (60 ml.) soft butter or
  margarine

4 tablespoons (60 ml.) honey
1⅓ cups (330 ml.) graham
  cracker crumbs

Cream together the butter and honey. Add the graham cracker crumbs and work in until crumbly. Press into a 9- or 10-inch (18- or 20-cm.) pie plate.

Bake at 375° for 8 minutes, or chill until set. Fill with a custard pudding or other desired filling.

Variation
(This recipe contains no wheat)
Substitute oatmeal cracker crumbs for the graham cracker crumbs.

FRUIT PIES

Make your favorite fruit pies, substituting ¾ cup (180 ml.) honey for 1 cup (250 ml.) sugar. The honey enhances the fruit flavor and less is needed than any sugar measure given in a recipe.

Also cut back on the total amount of sugar used in any pie, cake, or cookie recipe. Most recipes are much sweeter than necessary.

APPLE PIE

(For people over 12 months old, 1 10-inch or 20-cm. pie)

1 double-crust recipe for pastry
  (see pp. 170, 171)
4 cups (1 liter) thinly pared,
  cored, sliced apples
¾ cup (180 ml.) honey
1 teaspoon (5 ml.) ground

cinnamon with ¼ teaspoon (1
ml.) ground nutmeg or 1
teaspoon (5 ml.) ground allspice
or 1 teaspoon (5 ml.) ground
cloves
Butter or margarine

Line a pie plate with the pastry. Combine the apples with the honey and spices and pour into the pastry. Dot the apples with the butter. Place the top crust on the pie, and pinch the edges together. Cut slits in the top crust for steam to escape.

Bake at 450° for 10 minutes. Lower the oven temperature to 375° and bake for 40 minutes longer. Cool on rack before cutting.

Variations
Substitute other fruits for apples. Combine 3 to 4 tablespoons (45 to 60 ml.) flour or 1 tablespoon (15 ml.) quick-cooking tapioca or 2 tablespoons (30 ml.) cornstarch with the honey before adding the fruit. This is to thicken the juices.

Prepare and bake as above.

SQUASH OR PUMPKIN PIE

(For people over 12 months old, 1 10-inch or 20-cm. pie)

1½ cups (375 ml.) canned
  strained pumpkin or squash or
  fresh home-prepared pumpkin or
  squash, puréed
⅓ cup (80 ml.) honey
¼ teaspoon (1 ml.) ground ginger
¼ teaspoon (1 ml.) ground
  nutmeg

½ teaspoon (2 ml.) ground
  cinnamon
½ teaspoon (2 ml.) salt
2 tablespoons (30 ml.) unbleached,
  enriched all-purpose white flour
¼ cup (60 ml.) light corn syrup
2 eggs, well beaten
1¼ cups (310 ml.) milk

Heat the pumpkin or squash in a saucepan, stirring frequently to prevent scorching. Combine the honey, ginger, nutmeg, cinnamon, salt, and flour and add to the hot pumpkin or squash. Add the corn syrup, mixing thoroughly. Mix in well the beaten eggs, add the milk, and beat until smooth. Pour into the unbaked 10-inch (20-cm.) pie shell. Bake at 375° for 10 minutes. Lower the oven temperature to 325° and bake for 35 minutes longer, or until a knife inserted near the edge of the pie comes out clean. Let cool on a wire rack before serving.

SPREADS

APPLE BUTTER

(For people over 6 months old)

1 quart (1 liter) fresh, unpreserved sweet cider or unsweetened apple juice

4 quarts (4 liters) all purpose sweet apples (MacIntosh or Cortlands are excellent; do not use Delicious)

(2 tablespoons or 30 ml. lemon juice)

(1 tablespoon or 15 ml. ground cinnamon)

Boil the cider until you have reduced it to 1 pint. Quarter the apples, removing the stems and blossom ends. Add the apples to the reduced cider and simmer, covered, over low heat, stirring occasionally until the apples are tender. Put through a food mill to remove the cores and skins. Return to the heat and simmer, uncovered, until the apple butter has thickened to the consistency of marmalade. Stir occasionally. Up to 2 tablespoons (30 ml.) of lemon juice and/or 1 tablespoon (15 ml.) of ground cinnamon may be added about 15 minutes before the mixture has finished cooking (when it gets very thick and plops off a raised spoon).

Fill sterile jars, seal, and label.

This recipe makes about 1 quart (1 liter), but you can increase the recipe by as much as you wish. It is practically foolproof as long as you don't burn it. If you don't want to purée the apples, pare and core them prior to cooking. Use the skins and cores to make jelly.

BUTTERS FROM DRIED FRUITS

(For people over 6 months old)

Use any dried fruit or a mixture of dried fruit, such as apricots, peaches, pears, or prunes. Figs or dates may be added in small amounts for flavor and sweetening.

Using 2 pounds (1 kilogram) of dried fruit, add water until you can just see it through the fruit. Simmer, covered, until tender, stirring occasionally. (Remove prune pits.) Put through food mill, ricer, or sieve. Return to the pot and simmer until thick.

With some fruits, such as apricots, you may wish to add honey to sweeten. You may add 1 teaspoon (5 ml.) ground cinnamon, cloves, or allspice if desired for flavor. Fill sterile jars, seal, and label. Makes about 1½ pints (750 ml.).

PEAR BUTTER

(For people over 6 months old)

2 quarts (2 liters) quartered ripe soft pears
1 cup (250 ml.) water

(1 tablespoon or 15 ml. lemon juice)
(1 teaspoon or 5 ml. ground ginger)

Remove blossom ends and stems from the pears and quarter the pears. Put them in a heavy pot with the water. Bring to a boil over moderate heat, stirring occasionally. Put through a food mill to remove the cores and peels. Return to the heat and simmer, uncovered, until thick.

Add 1 tablespoon (15 ml.) of lemon juice and/or 1 teaspoon (5 ml.) of ground ginger, if desired, when the mixture thickens enough to plop off a raised spoon—about 15 minutes before removing from heat. Fill sterile jars, seal, and label. Makes about 1½ pints (750 ml.).

TOMATO MARMALADE

(For people over 12 months old)

1¼ pounds (625 g.) ripe tomatoes
½ medium-sized lemon
1 teaspoon (5 ml.) grated
gingerroot or chopped preserved

gingerroot or chopped preserved
ginger
1 pound (500 g.) honey

Scald, pare, and slice the tomatoes into a heavy non-aluminum pot. Add the very thinly sliced lemon or grated peel and juice. Add the ginger and simmer for 1 hour, stirring occasionally. Stir in the honey and bring to a boil, stirring constantly. Watch that the honey does not cause the mixture to boil over. Simmer until thick. Cool, and pour into sterile glasses, seal, and label. Makes about 1½ pints (750 ml.)

NUT OR SEED BUTTERS

(For people over 12 months old)
   Use peanuts, pecans, or walnuts. For seed butter, use choice of sesame, sunflower, or pumpkin seeds.
   Put 1 cup (250 ml.) fresh-roasted nuts or seeds in the container of a blender or food processor. If using a blender, add 2 to 4 tablespoons (30 to 60 ml.) oil. If using a food processor, oil is optional. Oil does make the process smoother and less sticky. Process on high speed until well-ground. For some seeds, you may need to use a nut grinder.

CARROT–PEANUT BUTTER SPREAD

Mix puréed cooked carrots with equal amounts of peanut butter.

FRUIT–PEANUT BUTTER SPREAD

Mix finely chopped dried fruit or cooked puréed fruit with an equal amount of peanut butter.

COTTAGE CHEESE–OLIVE SPREAD

(For people over 9 months old)
Blend 1 or 2 tablespoons (15 or 30 ml.) chopped or blended stuffed olives with 1 cup (250 ml.) creamed cottage cheese.

COTTAGE CHEESE–PINEAPPLE SPREAD

(For people over 9 months old)
Blend 1 cup (250 ml.) cottage cheese with ½ cup (125 ml.) crushed unsweetened pineapple.

Variation
Use other cooked fruits—apricots, applesauce, peaches—in place of the pineapple and make in the same way as the *Cottage Cheese-Pineapple Spread*.

SECTION 9:

EGGS

HARD-COOKED EGG YOLK FOR BABIES

Put the egg in a small saucepan with cold water to cover. (A dash of vinegar added to the water helps prevent the shell from breaking.) Bring the water to a boil and turn off the heat. Let sit for 20 minutes. Run under cold water to loosen the shell. Peel. For young babies, remove the yolk and mash. The whites may be used to garnish salads and other family foods.

Eggs ought not to be cooked with too much heat or the whites will toughen. Hard-cooked eggs, if cooked too long or over too high a flame, may have greenish yolks. Though they are not as attractive and may be a bit dry, they are perfectly edible.

As the baby grows older, raw yolk may be separated from white and poached in simmering water until set. Whites may then be used more efficiently in cooking for the family. To freeze for later use, mix egg whites with a pinch of salt.

Suggested uses for whites: meringues, angel cake, macaroons, baked fruit whip, or to replace whole eggs in almost any baked goods (as sometimes recommended for adults on a low-cholesterol diet).

A baby custard may be prepared from one egg yolk and ¼ cup (60 ml.) milk. Cook, covered, over simmering water until set.

POACHED EGGS

(For people over 12 months old)

Break the egg into a saucer. Slip into 1 inch (2 cm.) of simmering water in a small saucepan or skillet. Cook until the egg white is firm. The hot water may be gently spooned over the yolk to set the top, or the pan may be covered. Remove with slotted spoon and serve on buttered toast.

If you use an egg poaching pan, butter the poaching cup, break the egg into the cup, place over simmering water, cover, and cook until set.

SCRAMBLED EGGS

(For people over 12 months old)

Combine 1 tablespoon (15 ml.) milk with each egg (or use egg yolks only combined with milk or water in place of the white). Beat with a fork to break the yolk and mix in the milk.

Melt butter in a small skillet over low heat, add beaten eggs, stirring constantly.

Or melt 1 teaspoon (5 ml.) butter or margarine in the top of a double boiler. Cook over hot water, stirring just enough to prevent the egg from sticking. Cook until set but not tough.

Variation

For older people, add a little parsley, minced onion, chopped green pepper, grated cheese, or chopped vegetable for variety and flavor.

FRENCH TOAST

(For people over 12 months old, 1 serving)

1 egg or egg yolk
2 tablespoons (30 ml.) milk
(Pinch of salt)
Slice of bread

Combine the egg and milk (and salt) by stirring with a fork. Dip the bread in the egg mixture to coat. Sauté in butter or margarine over moderate heat on both sides until browned.

FRENCH TOAST SANDWICHES

(For people over 12 months old, 1 serving)
Blend 2 teaspoons (10 ml.) mashed fruit with 1 tablespoon (15 ml.) peanut butter. Spread on a slice of bread. Top with a second slice of bread. Dip in the egg mixture above. Sauté on both sides over moderate heat.

Or, put a thin slice of natural cheese between the bread slices. Dip in the egg mixture above and sauté over moderate heat.

Cut the sandwiches in ladyfingers to serve.

FOAMY OMELET

(For people over 12 months old, 2 toddler servings)

2 egg yolks	(Chopped parsley)
2 tablespoons (30 ml.) water	2 egg whites
(Pinch of salt)	1 tablespoon (15 ml.) butter or
(Pinch of ground pepper)	margarine

Beat the egg yolks with water (and salt, pepper, and parsley), until light and foamy. Beat the whites until stiff and fold into the yolks. Melt the butter or margarine in small skillet. Add the egg mixture and cook over low heat until light brown on the bottom. Bake in a 325° oven until set and dry on top, about 5 minutes.

Serve on a warm plate. Top the omelet with cheese sauce (see p. 190), tomatoes, or creamed vegetables as desired.

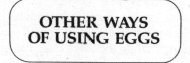

OTHER WAYS OF USING EGGS

Mashed hard-cooked egg yolks can be mixed with meat or vegetables if the baby does not find them palatable alone.

For older babies, mix the whole egg in one of the combination dinners or in a creamed soup. Be sure, if you add eggs to creamed soup or other hot dishes, that you beat the eggs first, stir a little of the hot mixture into the beaten eggs, and then, stirring constantly, add the eggs to the hot mixture.

You can use an egg to replace potato or flour as thickening.

SECTION 10:

MILK, CHEESE, YOGURT, PUDDINGS, AND CUSTARDS

COTTAGE CHEESE AND BUTTERMILK

Cottage cheese is an unripened, soft, natural cheese made from skimmed milk. Creamed cottage cheese has cream added to improve the flavor and consistency; consequently, it is higher in calories than the nonfat cottage cheese. Small curd cottage cheese is made without rennet, while the large curd has rennet added to it. Rennet is a natural enzyme which acts on milk to form curds. Italian cottage cheese is known as ricotta.

Cottage cheese should be used within 3 to 5 days. It is easy to make your own starting from buttermilk (see recipe below).

Buttermilk

For each quart of buttermilk you wish to make, add ½ cup (125 ml.) commercial buttermilk and a pinch of salt to 1 quart of reconstituted nonfat dry milk. Let stand at room temperature until clabbered (thick), about 24 hours. Refrigerate, or proceed with cottage cheese.

"Cultured Buttermilk Powder" is now available in many grocery stores. It can be used in any recipe calling for liquid buttermilk or sour milk, by adding the powder to the dry ingredients and substituting water for the liquid buttermilk called for. Four tablespoons (60 ml.) of buttermilk powder and 1 cup (250 ml.) of water replaces 1 cup of buttermilk or sour milk in a recipe.

Cottage Cheese

When the buttermilk curds are sufficiently thick to break cleanly away from the side of the pan, cut the curd into 1-inch (2.5-cm.) squares with a spatula or long knife. Place the pan over very low heat. (If you have a gas stove, you will probably need to place it in a pan of hot water, heating that.) Slowly heat the curds up to 120°. Stir gently until the curds are firm but not tough and have separated from the whey. Pour into a cheesecloth-lined strainer (or use a dish towel). Lift the edges of the cloth to help drain the whey off. Rinse the curd with water. Let drain. You may add salt and sweet or sour cream, if desired.

YOGURT

Yogurt is a highly digestible product of milk formed by the addition of a culture of *Lactobacillus bulgaricus.* (Buttermilk is cultured from the *Lactobacillus acidophilus*.) The culture of yogurt is a bit more exacting than that of buttermilk, but you can make a quart of yogurt at home from nonfat dry milk for about half what you would pay in the store.

Set the temperature of your electric fry pan to 100°. (The lowest temperature setting on the indicator may be higher than this, but you can judge the distance below that to approximately 100°.)

Use reconstituted nonfat dry milk, homogenized milk, fresh 2 percent or skimmed milk, or diluted evaporated milk. (Any of these may be further enriched by the addition of extra nonfat dry milk.)

For 1 quart (1 liter) of milk, add about 3 tablespoons (45 ml.) of yogurt. Fill four ½- to 1-pint (250- to 500-ml.) containers with the mixture. (Heat-resistant refrigerator dishes or the small stainless steel dishes that come with plastic covers are ideal containers.) Pour hot water (about 110°) into the electric fry pan. Place the containers of milk mixed with yogurt in the pan. Cover the pan and leave it undisturbed for 3 to 6 hours or longer. When the yogurt is thick and custardy, it is done.

Save some of your first batch for use in making the next batch.

The curds of buttermilk, cottage cheese, and yogurt are easily digested and well tolerated by babies.

Mix yogurt with fruit for baby's first dessert. You may wish to add 1 tablespoon (15 ml.) unflavored gelatin mixed with 3 table-spoons (45 ml.) boiling water to dissolve the gelatin. The gelatin sets the yogurt to a slightly firmer texture.

NATURAL HARD CHEESE

The hard cheeses, such as Cheddar, are formed by a process of coagulating the whole milk with rennet, pressing the separated curd, and ripening (aging) it.

Unfortunately, some natural hard cheeses now have preserva-tives added to them. This is especially true of those that are prepackaged by manufacturers or distributors. Those cut from the round or brick are usually free of preservatives. Check labels carefully to determine whether or not preservatives have been added.

The protein of natural cheese is a complete protein and can be used pound for pound to replace meat in a meal.

PASTEURIZED PROCESSED CHEESE

Pasteurized processed cheese is a blend of aged and fresh cheeses which have been melted, mixed with emulsifiers, and pasteurized. Obviously, the flavor tends to be bland, and since the ripening is stopped by pasteurization, that flavor remains the same for a long period of time. Processed cheeses have no waste, but you generally need to add more to impart the same amount of flavor that natural cheese has. This means that you may get less value for your dollar.

It is also common to find that they contain preservatives or other additives.

Pasteurized processed cheese food and cheese spreads are just more watered-down versions of processed cheeses. They have numerous additives, including gums, stabilizers, preservatives, a high water content, and less fat. As a result, many of them are as tasteless and as bland as wallpaper paste. Some have various spices, fruits, and vegetables added. One must read labels carefully since they often come packaged in slices that look identical to processed cheese slices although the product is inferior.

Cheese-type foods which are not up to government standards are called imitation cheese. In some cases the product is merely made without the fat content of natural cheese and, thus, may have a different texture. These imitation cheeses are replacing natural cheese more and more often in such processed foods as frozen pizza, macaroni and cheese, etc. What started as a product to be used in dietetic foods is now being used in many other foods because it results in a higher profit margin.

TOFU
(BEAN CURD)

Tofu is a cheese or curd made from soy milk. It is smooth-textured and has no real flavor of its own. It blends with and absorbs the flavor from the foods it is mixed with.

Tofu comes in various textures depending on the amount of water which is retained in it. Firm tofu can be sliced and fried or crumbled and added to salads. The softer tofu can be used to make soft spreads, custards, etc.

Tofu can be used to replace the ricotta cheese in Italian recipes or in place of cottage cheese or cream cheese. It is sold by the pound in many supermarkets, food co-ops, natural food stores, and Oriental grocery stores.

For directions on making your own tofu, see *The Farm Vegetarian Cookbook*, edited by Louise Hagler.

NATURAL CHEESE RECIPES

CHEESE SPREAD

(For people over 12 months old)

If you want a cheese spread, why not make your own? It will have more flavor and be far nearer purity than the packaged spreads you can buy.

½ cup (125 ml.) milk
1 egg, beaten
¾ pound (375 g.) Cheddar cheese, grated

(¼ teaspoon or 1 ml. dry mustard)
(½ teaspoon or 2 ml. salt)

Heat the milk in the top of a double boiler over hot water. Combine the egg and grated cheese (and dry mustard and salt). Add slowly to the milk, stirring constantly. Cook, stirring, for 15 minutes. Cool. Store in a covered jar in the refrigerator. This keeps for more than a week and makes an excellent cheese spread.

Variations

1. Add bits of crumbled crisp bacon.
2. Add 2 tablespoons (30 ml.) chopped pimientos.
3. Use tomato juice instead of milk.
4. Add ¼ teaspoon (1 ml.) caraway seeds, crumbled dried sage, or other spices as desired.
5. Add ⅛ teaspoon (.5 ml.) garlic powder or ¼ teaspoon (1 ml.) onion powder, in portions for older children and adults.

WELSH RAREBIT

(For people over 12 months old, 4 servings)

1 tablespoon (15 ml.) butter or
  margarine
1½ cups (375 ml.) diced natural
  cheese
⅔ cup (160 ml.) rich milk or
  partially diluted evaporated milk

(¼ teaspoon or 1 ml. salt)
(¼ teaspoon or 1 ml. dry
  mustard)
(1 teaspoon or 5 ml.
  Worcestershire sauce)
1 egg yolk, beaten

Melt the butter or margarine over hot water in the top of a double boiler. Stir in the cheese and milk. (Add salt, dry mustard, and Worcestershire sauce.) Stir until the cheese melts and the mixture is hot. Remove from the heat. Add a little of the mixture to the beaten egg yolk and return to the pot with the egg yolk. Stir. Serve over crackers or toast.

Variation
Use tomato juice in place of the milk.

CARROT CHEESE SOUFFLÉ

(For people over 12 months old, 5 servings)

2 teaspoons (10 ml.) butter or
  margarine
2 teaspoons (10 ml.) whole wheat
  or unbleached, enriched
  all-purpose white flour

¼ cup (60 ml.) whole milk
⅓ cup (80 ml.) grated mild
  natural cheese
¼ cup (60 ml.) strained carrots
2 eggs, separated

Melt the butter or margarine in a saucepan. Blend in the flour. Add the milk, stirring until the mixture is thick and smooth. Add the cheese and carrots. Gradually stir in the beaten egg yolks. Fold in the stiffly beaten egg whites. Pour into a buttered casserole or custard cups. Set in pan of hot water and bake at 325° for 50 minutes, or until the center is firm.

SPANISH RICE

(For people over 9 months old, 6 servings)

2 tablespoons (30 ml.) butter or
   margarine
(¼ cup or 60 ml. chopped green
   pepper)
(1 small onion, chopped)
3 cups (750 ml.) cooked brown
   rice

1 cup (250 ml.) peeled tomatoes,
   fresh or canned
(Salt and pepper to taste)
½ cup (125 ml.) grated natural
   cheese

Melt butter in large skillet. (Over moderate heat, sauté the onion and green pepper until onion is transparent but not brown.) Add the rice. Stir until heated through. Add the tomatoes (and seasonings) and pour into a buttered casserole. Add the cheese and stir. Bake at 375° for 20 minutes.

Variations
Add chopped cooked beef or crumbled ground beef with the onion and green pepper. Add ¼ cup (60 ml.) nonfat dry milk with the cheese.

This may be put into individual custard cups or casseroles, frozen, then thawed and heated until the cheese is melted.

BEEF AND CHEESE CASSEROLE

(For people over 12 months old, 4 to 6 servings)

½ pound (250 g.) ground beef
1 tablespoon (15 ml.) butter or
   margarine
2 cups (500 ml.) peeled tomatoes,
   fresh or canned
2 cups (500 ml.) cottage cheese
½ cup (125 ml.) sour cream

(½ or 125 ml. minced onion)
(1 tablespoon or 15 ml. chopped
   green pepper)
(Salt, pepper)
½ pound (250 g.) egg noodles,
   cooked

Cook the ground beef in butter or margarine until it is no longer red. Add the tomatoes and continue to cook until heated through or, if fresh, until tender. Combine the cheese and sour cream (and onion, green pepper, and seasonings). Layer half the noodles in the bottom of a buttered casserole. Add the cheese mixture. Make a layer with the remaining noodles. Spread the meat mixture on top. Bake at 375° for 20 to 30 minutes.

This may be frozen in individual custard cups or casseroles, then thawed and heated until the cheese is melted.

CREAM SAUCE

(For people over 9 months old, makes 1 cup or 250 ml.)

2 tablespoons (30 ml.) butter for light sauce, or 3 tablespoons (45 ml.) butter for thick sauce

1½ tablespoons (22 ml.) unbleached enriched all-purpose

white flour for light sauce, or 3 tablespoons (45 ml.) for a thicker sauce

1 cup (250 ml.) milk or stock (Salt and pepper to taste)

Melt the butter in heavy saucepan over moderate heat until it is bubbling but not brown. Remove the pan from the heat while stirring in flour. Return the pan to the heat and continue to stir while slowly adding the milk. Stir continuously until thickened. (Add salt and pepper to taste.)

Variation
(This recipe contains no wheat)
Use 1 tablespoon (15 ml.) cornstarch for a light sauce and 2 tablespoons (30 ml.) cornstarch for a thicker sauce in place of the flour called for.

CHEESE SAUCE

(For people over 12 months old, makes 1½ cups or 375 ml.)
Make a cream sauce as above. When hot, gradually stir in ½ cup (125 ml.) natural grated cheese, stirring until the cheese melts and the sauce is smooth.

COOKED EGGNOG

(For people over 12 months old)
Since uncooked egg white may be more liable to cause allergy and may interfere with the absorption of biotin (a member of the B complex of vitamins), eggnog should be cooked or made only of egg yolk. Because of the further danger of eggs being contaminated with salmonella, cooked eggnog is strongly recommended.

1 cup (250 ml.) milk   *(Pure vanilla extract and grated*
1 egg or egg yolk   *nutmeg)*
1 tablespoon (15 ml.) honey

Heat the milk and honey together over moderate heat to just below the boiling point. Beat the egg with a wire whisk. Add in a slow stream to the hot milk while beating constantly with the wire whisk. As soon as all the egg has been added, remove from the heat, cool, and chill. (Add the vanilla and grated nutmeg.) Extra nonfat dry milk powder and/or wheat germ may be added as desired.

When the eggnog is cold, ¼ cup (60 ml.) fruit may be blended into it, or ¼ cup (60 ml.) orange juice with ¼ cup (60 ml.) cooked carrots.

MILK SHAKES

These are simple to make in a blender. If you do not have a blender, most milk shakes can be made with an egg beater or an electric mixer. Made with honey, these are suitable for babies over 12 months old. For younger people, eliminate the honey or substitute light corn syrup for the sweetener.

All of these variations yield 1 or 2 servings.

1. 1 cup (250 ml.) milk, 2 tablespoons (30 ml.) peanut butter, 1 teaspoon (5 ml.) honey, fresh or dried fruit as desired
2. 1 cup (250 ml.) milk, ½ teaspoon (2 ml.) honey, (pinch cinnamon), (pinch nutmeg)
3. 1 cup (250 ml.) milk, 1 tablespoon (15 ml.) molasses
4. 1 cup (250 ml.) milk, ½ cup (125 ml.) fresh, cooked, or dried fruit, honey to taste
5. ¾ cup (180 ml.) milk, ½ large or 1 small banana, 1 tablespoon (15 ml.) honey
6. 1 cup (250 ml.) milk, 4 pitted cooked prunes, ½ cup (125 ml.) prune juice, 1 teaspoon (5 ml.) honey

CARROT VELVET

(For people over 12 months old)
Blend together until smooth 1 cup (250 ml.) milk, ⅔ cup (160 ml.) cooked or canned carrots, 1 tablespoon (15 ml.) orange juice, 2 teaspoons (10 ml.) honey, and 1 scoop vanilla ice cream or ice milk (and a pinch of salt and a pinch of ground nutmeg).

FRUIT AND NUT SHAKE

(For people over 12 months old)
Blend 2 cups (500 ml.) milk, a peach, a banana, 2 pitted dates, and 2 tablespoons (30 ml.) almonds for each 2 to 3 servings.

PUDDINGS
AND CUSTARDS

FRUIT GELATIN

(For people over 6 months old, 3 ½-cup or 60 ml. servings)

Soak 1 tablespoon (15 ml.) unflavored gelatin in ¼ cup (60 ml.) water or juice in a cup. Set the cup in hot water to dissolve the gelatin. Cool slightly and add to 1¼ cups (310 ml.) fruit juice or 1½ cups (375 ml.) fruit purée. Refrigerate until firm.

Variations

(For people over 12 months old)

When gelatin is partially set, fold in a choice of:

1. ½ cup (125 ml.) cottage cheese
2. ½ cup (125 ml.) grated carrots and ¼ cup (60 ml.) raisins
3. ½ cup (125 ml.) raw, grated or scraped apple, pears, mashed bananas, or other fruits

WHIPS OR CHIFFONS

Prepare the gelatin recipe. When nearly set, whip until foamy. You may fold in whipped chilled evaporated milk or whipped nonfat dry milk (made of ½ cup or 125 ml. nonfat dry milk powder in ½ cup or 125 ml. ice water).

This yields 6 or 8 servings depending on amount of gelatin recipe.

BAKED FRUIT WHIP

(For people over 12 months old, 1 or 2 servings)

1 egg white
(Pinch of salt)
2 tablespoons (30 ml.) honey

1 tablespoon (15 ml.) lemon juice
½ cup (125 ml.) puréed fruit

Beat the egg white (with salt) until stiff but not dry. Gradually add the honey as you beat. Add the lemon juice to the fruit and fold the fruit into the egg white mixture. Turn into an oiled baking dish. Set in pan of hot water. Bake at 300° until the center is firm, about 50 minutes.

FRUIT CRUNCH

(For people over 9 months old, 2 servings)

¾ cup (180 ml.) cooked mashed
  or puréed fruit
3 tablespoons (45 ml.) wheat germ
3 tablespoons (45 ml.) brown
  sugar

1½ tablespoons (22 ml.) butter or
  margarine
(Pinch of ground cinnamon)

Put the fruit into a small greased baking dish. Blend the wheat germ, brown sugar, and butter or margarine (and cinnamon). Sprinkle over the fruit.
Bake at 350° until hot and nicely browned, about 20 minutes.

Variation
Use crumbs of two graham crackers or oat crackers for topping.

STOVE–TOP CUSTARD

(For people over 12 months old, 5 servings)

3 tablespoons (45 ml.) honey
½ cup (125 ml.) nonfat dry milk
  powder
(Pinch of salt)

½ cup (125 ml.) fresh milk
2 whole eggs or 4 egg yolks
1½ cups (375 ml.) fresh milk
(1 teaspoon or 5 ml. vanilla)

Combine the honey and nonfat dry milk powder (and salt) in a heavy saucepan. Add ½ cup (125 ml.) fresh milk and the eggs. Beat thoroughly and add the remaining milk.

Cook over moderate heat, stirring constantly for about 4 minutes. (Add the vanilla.) Chill.

Variation

Add fruit after cooking the custard.

BAKED CUSTARD

(For people over 9 months old, 4 servings)

1 cup (250 ml.) milk
1 egg or 2 egg yolks
2 tablespoons (30 ml.) honey

¼ teaspoon (1 ml.) vanilla
(Pinch of salt)

This is the basic recipe, but multiply it as many times as you wish. If you have a blender, blend the milk, egg, honey, and vanilla (and salt) until smooth. Or beat vigorously by hand. Pour into custard cups, and set them in a pan of hot water.

Bake at 325° for 1 hour, or until a knife inserted near the edge of a cup comes out clean. Chill at once.

Variations

1. Add 2 tablespoons (30 ml.) wheat germ for each cup (250 ml.) of milk.

2. Add 1 tablespoon (15 ml.) raisins.

3. Add ½ cup (125 ml.) cooked rice with a pinch of ground cinnamon and 1 tablespoon (15 ml.) raisins.

RICE PUDDING

(This recipe contains no eggs)
(For people over 9 months old, 6 to 8 servings)

¼ cup (60 ml.) rice
2 cups (500 ml.) milk
¼ cup (60 ml.) molasses

(¼ teaspoon or 1 ml. ground
  cinnamon)
(Pinch of salt)

Combine the rice, milk, and molasses (and cinnamon and salt) in a buttered baking dish. Bake at 325° for 2½ hours, stirring occasionally.

INDIAN PUDDING

(This recipe contains no eggs)
(For people over 9 months old, 6 to 8 servings)

¼ cup (60 ml.) undegerminated
  cornmeal
2 cups (500 ml.) hot milk
⅛ teaspoon (.5 ml.) baking soda
(½ teaspoon or 2 ml. salt)
(½ teaspoon or 2 ml. ground
  ginger)

(½ teaspoon or 2 ml. ground
  cinnamon)
½ cup (125 ml.) molasses
1 cup (250 ml.) cold milk

Gradually add the cornmeal to the hot milk, stirring constantly. Cook over low heat for 15 minutes, or until thick. Mix the baking soda (and salt, ginger, and cinnamon) into the cornmeal mixture. Add the molasses and cold milk. Pour into a 1-quart (1-liter) casserole or baking dish. Bake at 275° for 2 hours.

BLENDER SWEET POTATO PUDDING

(For people over 12 months old, 6 servings)

3 eggs
¾ cup (180 ml.) molasses
½ cup (125 ml.) milk
½ cup (125 ml.) butter or
  margarine, melted

½ teaspoon (2 ml.) ground
  nutmeg
(½ teaspoon or 2 ml. salt)
3½ cups (875 ml.) cut-up raw
  sweet potatoes

Put in blender or food processor: eggs, molasses, milk, melted butter or margarine, nutmeg, (salt), and 1 cup (250 ml.) of the cut-up raw sweet potatoes. Cover and process until smooth.

Remove the cover and gradually add, while blending, the remaining 2½ cups (625 ml.) sweet potatoes. Pour into a buttered baking dish. Add ½ cup (125 ml.) raisins, if you wish, or for adults and older children, ½ cup (125 ml.) ground nuts. Bake at 325° for 1½ hours.

COTTAGE CHEESE CAKE

(For people over 12 months old, 1 9-inch or 18 cm. cake)

1½ cups (375 ml.) crushed
  graham crackers
⅓ cup (80 ml.) soft butter or
  margarine
½ cup (125 ml.) honey
3 egg whites
½ pound (1 cup, 250 g./ml.)
  drained, packed cottage cheese

1 tablespoon (15 ml.) additional
  butter or margarine
3 tablespoons (45 ml.) cornstarch
1 cup (250 ml.) buttermilk
3 egg yolks, slightly beaten
1 teaspoon (5 ml.) vanilla

Mix the graham cracker crumbs and softened butter or margarine with ¼ cup (60 ml.) honey. Press most of the crumbs into a 9-inch (18-cm.) cake or pie pan; save 2 tablespoons (30 ml.) for the topping.

Beat the egg whites until stiff. Beat the cottage cheese with the remaining 1 tablespoon (15 ml.) butter or margarine, cornstarch, and the remaining honey until light. Add the buttermilk, egg yolks, and vanilla. Beat until smooth. Fold in the beaten egg whites. Pour into the prepared pan. Sprinkle the top with the reserved crumbs.

Bake at 400° for 25 minutes. Reduce the oven temperature to 325° and bake for 15 minutes longer, or until a knife inserted in the center comes out clean. Chill immediately .

THANKSGIVING PUDDING

(This recipe contains no eggs)
(For people over 12 months old, 12 servings)

⅔ cup (160 ml.) butter or
   margarine
1 cup (250 ml.) molasses
1 cup (250 ml.) sour milk or
   buttermilk
1 cup (250 ml.) chopped raisins or
   currants
2 cups (500 ml.) unbleached,
   enriched all-purpose white flour

¼ cup (60 ml.) soy flour
¼ cup (60 ml.) nonfat dry milk
   powder
2 teaspoons (10 ml.) wheat germ
1 teaspoon (5 ml.) baking soda
(½ teaspoon or 2 ml. salt)
(¼ teaspoon or 1 ml. ground
   nutmeg)
1 teaspoon (4 ml.) lemon juice

Cream the butter or margarine with molasses until light. Add the sour milk or buttermilk and chopped raisins. Combine the flours, dry milk powder, wheat germ, and baking soda (and salt and nutmeg). Stir into the molasses and sour milk mixture. Add the lemon juice.

Place in a greased 2-pound (1-kg.) coffee can or other 2-pound mold. Cover tightly with oiled brown paper. Set in a large pot. Add boiling water to the pot to come halfway up the mold. Cover tightly. Bring to a boil and steam for 3 hours, adding more boiling water to the pot as necessary. Unmold and serve warm with custard or cream.

BANANA-DATE PUDDING OR PIE

(This recipe contains no eggs, wheat, or milk)
(For people over 12 months old, 6 to 8 servings)

½ cup (125 ml.) chopped dates
½ cup (125 ml.) cashew pieces
3 cups (750 ml.) water
½ cup (125 ml.) cornstarch

½ cup (125 ml.) coconut, grated
(¼ teaspoon or 1 ml. salt)
4 ripe bananas
1 teaspoon (5 ml.) vanilla

Blend the dates and cashew pieces with the water until well liquefied. Stir a little of the liquid into the cornstarch to form a paste. Gradually stir in the remaining liquid until well blended. Add the coconut (and salt). Cook over medium heat in a heavy saucepan until the mixture thickens, just to the boiling point. Remove from the heat and cool slightly. Mash two of the bananas and add to the pudding with the vanilla. Cool to room temperature. For a pudding, spoon into serving dishes and slice the remaining bananas over the pudding. For a pie, slice the remaining bananas into the bottom of a baked 9-inch (18-cm.) pie shell. Spoon the pudding over the bananas. Chill. If not allergic to milk, serve with a yogurt topping.

BLENDER FROZEN FRUIT CREAM

(For people over 9 months old, 6 servings)

⅔ cup (160 ml.) evaporated milk
1 10-ounce (300 g.) package
  frozen, unsweetened fruit

Blend until smooth. Pour into an ice cube tray and freeze.

YOGURT SHERBET

(For people over 9 months old, 4 servings)

1 pint (500 ml. or 2 cups) yogurt
2 cups (500 ml.) fresh mashed,
blended, or grated fruit

Light corn syrup or honey to
sweeten

Freeze the yogurt to a soft mush. Remove from the freezer and beat well. Blend with the fruit and sweeten to taste. Return to the freezer.

This recipe may be used for a yogurt pudding by just mixing the ingredients, using chilled yogurt, and serving.

YOGURT POPSICLES

(For people over 12 months old, 8 servings)

1 pint (500 ml. or 2 cups) yogurt
2 tablespoons (30 ml.) light corn
syrup

1 cup (250 ml.) fresh mashed,
blended, or grated fruit
(⅛ teaspoon or .5 ml. ground
nutmeg)

Freeze the yogurt to a soft mush. Remove from the freezer and beat well. Add the corn syrup and fruit (and nutmeg) and beat at high speed.

Pour into eight popsicle molds. (Popsicle molds are available in houseware stores, or you can make your own out of small paper cups with a plastic spoon inserted in each to act as a stick. Insert the spoon only after the contents are half-frozen so that it will stand upright. Or make tiny popsicles in ice cube trays with plastic stirrers for sticks.)

Freeze until firm. To serve, peel away the paper cup or set mold or ice cube tray in pan of warm water for a few seconds to loosen the popsicles and make them slide out easily.

PINEAPPLE SHERBET

(For people over 9 months old, 4 servings)

Blend 1 can frozen unsweetened pineapple chunks until they are the consistency of smooth, creamy sherbet. (You can buy a can of unsweetened pineapple chunks and freeze it unopened.)

Variation

Use same recipe with packages of other types of frozen fruits.

ORANGE-PINEAPPLE FREEZE

(For people over 9 months old, 4 servings)

½ cup (125 ml.) hot orange juice
1 tablespoon (15 ml.) lemon juice
1 envelope unflavored gelatin
⅓ cup (80 ml.) honey
2 sliced bananas

½ cup (125 ml.) fresh orange or
    tangerine sections with
    membrane removed, or canned
    mandarin orange sections
1 cup (250 ml.) whipping cream

Put the hot orange juice, lemon juice, and unflavored gelatin in the container of a blender. Cover and blend. Add the honey, bananas, and orange sections. Blend until smooth. Whip the cream and fold into the mixture. Pour into an ice cube tray and freeze.

RESOURCES

BOOKS

Brewer, Gail Sforza. *What Every Pregnant Woman Should Know: The Truth about Diet and Drugs in Pregnancy.* New York: Random House, 1977.

Brewster, Dorothy Patricia. *You Can Breastfeed Your Baby . . . Even in Special Situations.* Emmaus, Pennsylvania: Rodale, 1979.

Crook, William G. *Can Your Child Read? Is He Hyperactive?* Jackson, Tennessee: Professional Books, rev. ed., 1977.

Ewald, Ellen B. *Recipes for a Small Planet.* New York: Ballantine, 1975.

Feingold, Benjamin. *Why Your Child Is Hyperactive.* New York: Random House, 1974.

Goldbeck, Nikki and David Goldbeck. *The Supermarket Handbook.* New York: New American Library, Signet Expanded Edition, 1976.

Hagler, Louise, ed. *The Farm Vegetarian Cookbook.* Summertown, Tennessee: The Book Publishing Co., rev. ed., 1978.

Hall, Ross Hume. *Food for Nought.* New York, Random House, 1976.

Hurd, Frank and Rosalie Hurd. *Ten Talents Cookbook: Vegetarian Natural Foods.* Chisholm, Minnesota: Ten Talents, 1968.

Klaus, Marshall H. and John H. Kennell. *Maternal-Infant Bonding.* St. Louis: C. V. Mosby, 1976.

La Leche League International. *The Womanly Art of Breastfeeding.* Franklin Park, Illinois, updated since 1958.

Lappe, Frances Moore. *Diet for a Small Planet.* New York: Ballantine, 1975.

Longacre, Doris. *More-With-Less Cookbook.* Scottsdale, Pennsylvania: Herald Press, 1976.

Pryor, Karen. *Nursing Your Baby.* New York: Harper and Row, 1973.

203

Smith, Lendon. *Feed Your Kids Right*. New York: McGraw-Hill, 1979.

Williams, Phyllis S. *Nourishing Your Unborn Child*, New York: Avon, 1976.

Yntema, Sharon. *Vegetarian Baby*. Ithaca, New York: McBooks, 1980.

ORGANIZATIONS

Center for Science in the Public Interest
1755 S Street
Washington, DC 20009

Children's Foundation
1420 New York Avenue, Room 800
Washington, DC 20025

Concern, Inc.
2233 Wisconsin Avenue NW
Washington, DC 20007

Food Research and Action Center
2011 I Street
Washington, DC 20006

Infant Formula Action Coalition (INFACT)
1701 University Avenue SE
Minneapolis, MN 55414

International Childbirth Education Association
P.O. Box 20048
Minneapolis, MN 55420

La Leche League International
2616 Minneapolis Avenue
Franklin Park, IL 60131

National Child Nutrition Project
303 George Street
New Brunswick, NJ 08901

Resources in Human Nurturing
3885 Forest Street/P.O. Box 6861
Denver, CO 80206

Society for the Protection of the Unborn Through Nutrition (SPUN)
17 North Wabash, Suite 603
Chicago, IL 60602

INDEX

A

Abbott Laboratories, formula manufacturer, 22
Additives, in food, 11–12, 67, 114
American Academy of Pediatrics, recommendations, 7, 14, 15, 29, 35–36
American Dietetic Association, 101
American Home Products, formula manufacturer, 22
Anderson, Dr. Thomas A., 9, 86
Allergies, 88–96
  case study of, 91–93
  chronic illness and, 91
  cooking and, 89, 95
  to eggs, 41–42, 89, 95
  hyperactivity and, 94
  to milk, 17, 29, 88–89, 95
  prevention of, 27, 89–94
  types of, 88–89
  vitamins and, 90
  to wheat, 90–91, 95–96
Apple, see also fruits
  apple butter, 174
  applesauce cake, 166
  fresh applesauce with pineapple, 122
  in infant diet, 50, 121
  pie, 166
  starting, 40

B

Baby foods
  best
    desserts, 48
    fish, 45–46
    fruits, 47
    grains and cereals, 48
    juices, 47
    legumes, 46–47
    meats and poultry, 45
    nonmeat main dishes, 46
    sources of calcium, 49
    sources of iron, 48–49
    spreads and pastes, 48
    vegetables, 46–47
  commercial, 4–12
    changes in, 4–10
    cleanliness of, 5
    disadvantages of, 10–12
    variety in, 10
  home-cooked
    advantages of, 9–13
    attacks on, 6–7
    cleanliness of, 5, 69–70
    preparation of, 70–75
    starting, 35–44, 78
    taste and texture of, 13, 79
Baby Keith, case study on infant obesity, 85–86
Banana, see also fruits
  bread, 161
  –date pudding or pie, 198
  in infant diet, 50, 143
  starting, 38
Beech-Nut Foods Corporation, baby food manufacturer, 4, 6–7, 9, 22
Beef, see also meat
  –and cheese casserole, 188–189
  –and kidney loaf, 132
  –and kidney stew, 132
  –and liver loaf, 131
Beutler, Ernest, on iron cookware, 72
Biscuits, 151
  rolled oat, 152
  teething, 150
Blenders and food processors, 70–71
  blender frozen fruit cream, 198
  blender sweet potato pudding, 196

209

212

215

W

Water
  in baby food, 11
  in formula, 18, 30, 33
  safety of, 116
Weight gain, *see also* obesity, over-
    feeding
  while breastfeeding, 19–20
  in infancy
    average, 79–80
    breastfeeding and, 83–84
    health and development and,
        84–85, 87
    trends, 84
  during pregnancy, 107–110
Welsh rarebit, 187
Wheat, *see also* breads, cereals,
    flours, grains
  allergy to, 90–91, 95–96
  substitutes for, 95–96
Whips or chiffons, 192
    see also puddings, sherbets
        and ice creams

baked fruit whip, 193
Wieloszynski, Roberta, on Beech-
    Nut controversy, 7
Womanly Art of Breastfeeding, The,
    24
World Health Organization, 22
Wurster, Charles F., on DDT in
    human milk, 115
Wynick, Dr. Myron, on infant
    growth patterns, 37

Y

Yntema, Sharon, *Vegetarian Baby*,
    105
Yogurt, 183–184
  best, 48
  popsicles, 199
  sherbet, 199
You Can Breastfeed Your Baby, 24

Z

Zweiback, 150